THE DOLPHIN'S BOY

Abid'allah, a Bedouin boy, was left deaf after falling out of a tree at the age of five. He became a mute loner, who spent much of his time swimming in the Red Sea. One day a female dolphin joined him — and from then on never left his side. This was remarkable, for dolphins usually prefer to live in groups. Day after day, Abid'allah swam and dived with his new friend, fished with her, and grew up alongside her. Then, something even more miraculous took place: Abid'allah began to talk. Their story has attracted scientists, film crews and journalists from around the world, but this is the only book to explore this remarkable friendship.

Pascale Noa Bercovitch is a journalist and documentary film director. She is an expert on the life of the Sinai desert, and divides her time between Israel and France. Handicapped herself, her unique telling of this story — which brings Egyptian, Israeli and Bedouin cultures together with that of the natural world — was made possible through the trust and friendship of Abid'allah and his tribe. She has also made a film about Abid'allah and Olin.

PASCALE NOA BERCOVITCH
Translated by STEVE COX

◆

THE
DOLPHIN'S BOY

A Story of Courage and Friendship

Complete and Unabridged

ULVERSCROFT
Leicester

First published in English in 2000 by
Sidgwick & Jackson
an imprint of
Macmillan Publishers Limited
London

First Large Print Edition
published 2001
by arrangement with
Macmillan Publishers Limited
London

The moral right of the author has been asserted

Translation by Steve Cox copyright
© Macmillan General Books 2000

Copyright © 1999 by Editions Robert Laffont
All rights reserved

British Library CIP Data

Bercovitch, Pascale Noa
    The dolphin's boy: a story of courage and friendship.
    —Large print ed.—
    Ulverscroft large print series: non-fiction
    1. Dolphins—Red Sea 2. Human-animal relationships
    —Red Sea 3. Large type books
    I. Title
    599.5′3′0916533

    ISBN 0–7089–4469–8

Published by
F. A. Thorpe (Publishing)
Anstey, Leicestershire

Set by Words & Graphics Ltd.
Anstey, Leicestershire
Printed and bound in Great Britain by
T. J. International Ltd., Padstow, Cornwall

This book is printed on acid-free paper

To my friend Joe Shoham, whose
memory goes with me.

To my friends Aharon and Hassida
Davidi, Sasson and Daisy Levy, and
Josiane Sarah Taieb, who knew how to
help me when I needed it.

In the reign of the divine Augustus, a dolphin entered Lake Lucrinus; a poor child who was walking from his home in Baia to Pozzoli to attend the primary school there gave it the name of Simon. No matter how far down it lay hidden, the animal would surface from the deep and . . . offer him its back to ride on . . . it carried him thus for several years, until the day when the boy from Naples died of an illness; the dolphin kept returning to the customary place, sorrowful, and showing signs of distress. In its turn, it let itself die of grief.

— Pliny the Elder,
Natural History, IX, 8

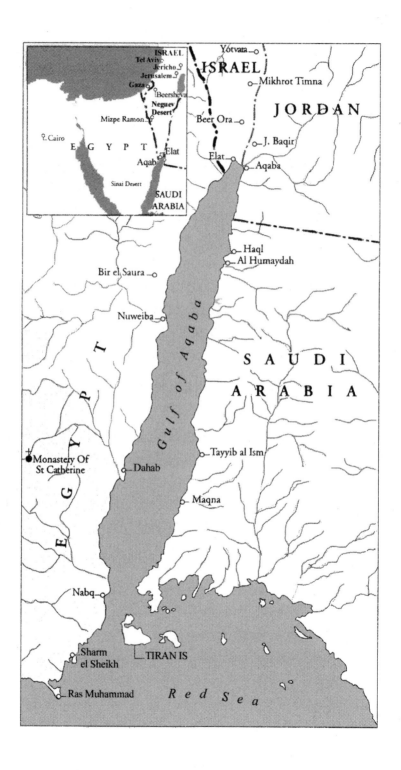

Where the desert meets the sea

Negev Desert, summer 1996

I drove slowly along the rambling road's sand-grey asphalt. The dust cloud behind me hovered in the wing-mirror, pursuing me like a manta ray, but it was the wavering path of the flying carpet of the sea that dictated the direction of my car.

Farmland, trees and signposted roads disappeared. I'd hit the desert — I could tell by the wind. Its breath changes, carrying off the past, both ill feelings and the best of memories. It forces me into the presence of the moment.

The sound that surrounded me was the desert's own. It's a pregnant silence. In it you hear the breathing of the earth, but also sometimes in the distance a tinkling, something like a little merry-go-round of wooden horses, that quickly fades. Maybe it's the sound of the stars that twinkle behind the daylight. The desert seems to have its own laws of physics, a nationality all its own.

I stopped to refuel and bought a carton of chocolate milk. The service station was like a port, a port on the high seas where the wind throws all the moorings, the scraps of metal, against the walls and signposts. The couplings rattled on the masts the way they do in all the harbours of the world, and the quiet, mingled delight of being nowhere flowed inside me.

★　★　★

People often believe that the desert is big: a crushing vastness, the same to the edge of infinity, a sun of blazing mercury that wraps up life and carries it away, a time counted only in centuries. But for me, the desert is nothing of the kind.

When I'm in the desert, I actually regain my sense of place as a human being, because the desert consists of nothing but the infinitely small. Its time is counted only in moments. Each one is unique, rich and full, spreading like a quiet tide, a patch of petrol or a handful of dough. Who can write a timetable in this kind of place, or specify a given hour or week? And the unexpected lurks in every nook and cranny. From a distance, these may all seem dull and flat . . . but they are the opposite. Nothing there is truly calculable. The further your journey proceeds, the more your rhythms work in harmony with it. You don't compel the desert:

2

it is its nature that rules. Its energy becomes yours if you respect it. It is as alive as you are.

★ ★ ★

As I was driving, I thought about the friendship between dolphins and men, which has to do with this same sense of being truly alive. It is for a dolphin that I was there, bound for Nuweiba el Muzeina, a Bedouin village on the far side of this desert, on the western shore of the Gulf of Elat.

The week before, Shlomo, a producer friend, had invited me to a funky café in Tel Aviv and told me about what he had seen in that village. For ten years, Shlomo has been in touch with a young deaf man called Abid'allah, who has struck up a kind of friendship with a wild Red Sea dolphin he calls Olin. Since then, Shlomo has distinctly heard him speak. I know he means it. 'It's a hell of a story!' he told me. 'Do you realize, this young guy was totally mute, he meets a dolphin, and now he talks and everyone comes to listen? Can you believe it? It's crazy!' He talked about it as though it was a miracle. This I do not understand: Sinai is a magical place, but to see miracles there is something else again. But his story intrigued me. What goes on between this boy and this animal, to fascinate Shlomo so much? He knows about my work making documentary films, and especially about my love of the Sinai and its desert, and my passion for Red Sea diving.

So he set to work persuading me to research the story of the dolphin Olin and his friend Abid'allah in order to make a film. I said yes.

★ ★ ★

I was burning up the kilometres, but felt as if was running on the spot. I passed a few military jeeps, with their infantry in outsize helmets draped with camouflage. Like alien tourists from another planet, they spend as much time in the dunes as the long-horned ibexes, strange inhabitants of this strange mountainscape of rocks and ghosts.

Heading due south means catching up with memories. When I was eighteen I entered the Sinai for the first time, already awed by its magic, though not understanding all its riches. All I had expected was to find another, foreign land, and it was only after spending time there and abandoning myself to its special 'passing of time' that I was able to capture the truth underlying Sinai.

This is a land made of distance, light and

4

time. And as with a camera shot, if you forget any one of these three factors, nothing happens. I now realize that Sinai is a cinema that never closes. The shows aren't free: you must earn your entrance by learning how to see and hear. To do this, you have to leave your usual sense of control at the gateway to the desert, in the same way as you take off your shoes at the entrance to a mosque.

★   ★   ★

I usually take the highway that runs north — south through the Araba Valley, through Beersheba, the city of the seven wells and the desert's only university, through the wind-swept ghost town of Mitzpe Ramon and the big Yotvata kibbutz.

After four hours of this steep route high above sea-level, I looked down at the Gulf of Elat. Here the Red Sea starts to reveal itself — in Hebrew, the Sea of Reeds, a tropical sea in the heart of one of the world's most arid regions.

Like an invitation, the sea laps against the beaches and hotel fences. Its legendary blue lurks between the little sailing ports and concrete jetties. It blesses Elat — more a seaside resort than a proper town — with the reflections of the mountains that surround it.

Crimson, red or pink, it is the same light that bathes Elat's sister town of Aqaba, in Jordan, further east. Today, thanks to the peace accords, everybody is free to travel in safety from one to the other, along the sea shore.

In Elat, I caught up with an old friend, Asher Gal, a scuba-diving instructor and sculptor. Till April 1982, while the Israelis were occupying Sinai, Asher was one of the pioneer agriculturists who built farms and fields in the middle of the desert. Using an efficient irrigation system, he grew melons for export. It went fine until the day came when he had to obey the bilateral accord that called for evacuating Sinai. Asher and all his friends on the moshav, the collective settlement, were broken-hearted.

But since then he has often returned to Nuweiba el Muzeina, where he meets the Bedouin friends who worked with him on the farm. And he saw the birth of young Abid'allah, the boy at the heart of the dolphin miracle story. I ask him to introduce us.

★ ★ ★

Happy to be back in each other's company, we drove fast along the coast into the Sinai. We passed through Taba and the Egyptian frontier with its customs officers in their odds and ends of faded official uniforms, which go with all their obsolete red tape, slightly threatening, like all state record systems. Rubber stamps, personal questions, smiles aimed at pretty girls who feel uncomfortable. Rough voices, whispered remarks, power at the end of an unloaded rusty rifle.

Eastwards, an endless beach follows the road. It protects the coral reef of the Red Sea. As we followed the coast, buildings emerged from the hillsides, with concrete arches and patterns of regular shadowed alcoves, springing up along the beaches. These are new hotels, huts and tourist centres, all built to house the visitors from all over the world who come in growing numbers to discover this little land of marvels.

Flashes of yellow and red turned out to be the helmets of the workmen, returning to their quarters in single file before nightfall. I thought they would be dejected, with their hard daily slog under the blazing sun, carrying the loneliness of immigrant workers whose family usually consists of dog-eared photos taped up over their camp-beds. Yet they seemed at ease in their dusty overalls, and there were smiles in their eyes. Maybe it was having the good fortune to be putting up these luxury buildings by the seaside, or to have any work at all in a country bled white by poverty. We exchanged the customary greetings. As my eyes followed them, in my heart I felt a pang of regret, and I hoped that this Sinai, which has changed so much since I first knew it, would keep its faith in simplicity and its own distinctive style.

In the time of the Israelis, this place was empty and enchanting. Only a few loin-clothed hippies, scuba enthusiasts, Israeli farmers and Bedouins — the ancestral inhabitants of the area — roamed its hills and strolled on its virgin beaches. Since 1982 and the restoration of these lands to the Egyptians, foreign investors have developed the Sinai peninsula and enhanced its value as a favourite tourist site. But in spite of the concrete and the tourists, we were still in Bedouin country.

We came to the port of Nuweiba, an old coastal outpost that contains the separate villages of two rival Bedouin tribes: Tarabine, which has always had outside visitors, and Muzeina, my own much less popular destination, just to the south.

The place is a stopping place for liners plying between Jordan, Saudi Arabia and the countries to the south of the Red Sea — Yemen, Djibouti ... The engineers and dockers there are Egyptians, from Cairo or Nubia; a long way from home, they play backgammon, smoke waterpipes, or watch TV in Arabic or Turkish, on battered sets with grey or fuzzy pictures. They eat in big open-air cafés, with small tables spaced out between barbecues, gigantic portraits of President Mubarak, and chunks of meat on spits. They also sell *fatir*, irresistible flaky coconut pastries.

Asher and I took a seat on the bistro-style wooden chairs. I sipped my squeezed lemon juice and offered a little prayer to be spared from the classic upset stomach. Egyptians are the most considerate people, but they have no idea how unhealthy their tap water is, having had their whole lives to get used to it.

I was the only woman there, but no one was shocked by my presence — on the contrary, I was treated like an honoured guest. In my many trips to Arab countries I have often noticed the great respect that men display to women, or at any rate to those who observe the minimal dress code: shoulders and knees covered, and a polite way of speaking, are usually adequate.

The Egyptian patissier asked me a few questions about where I come from and what I was doing there, at the dockside, and I told him about the miracle performed by Olin the dolphin. 'Never heard of it — you're sure, just a few kilometres south of here?' His Egyptian

Arabic was sweet as honey. Of course, he had no way of knowing. The Bedouins who come to enjoy his doughnuts don't talk about their lives, and tourists probably feel uneasy at the sight of these masses of men, dirty by day and clean at night, who eat here like the garrison of an imaginary army off duty. 'But I've heard another story,' he said.

'The Egyptians in Nuweiba talk about it. It happened, not last year but the year before. Some pilgrims on the Haj were on their way from Port Sudan to Mecca on one of the big ferries that stop over here.' He was referring to the liners that shuttle from one shore to the other of the Red Sea to carry the faithful on the annual pilgrimage to Saudi Arabia. 'One of them sank outside Port Sudan, several kilometres off the coast. It happened very fast, at dusk, they say, after Sha'am Rumi, and the depth at that point is over a thousand metres. Well, men were starting to scream. Others were drowning already, and they felt the waves sweeping them towards the rocks. You'll never guess what happened ... ' Caught by the story, and breathing the smoke from the sweet pancakes he was frying, I pressed him to continue.

'*Yallah, emshi!*' He stopped kneading for a moment and looked me straight in the eye: 'Dolphins, hundreds, this big!' He drew broad shapes in the sultry air, and started working again. 'Dolphins kept the survivors afloat and saved their lives. *Allah Akbar!* No one had ever seen such a miracle, they would all have died if Allah had not sent his creatures.'

My first story about Red Sea dolphins. It was confirmed for me later by Bedouins in Muzeina and by many others. Dolphins have always been very common here, and have never been hunted. They are respected or ignored by all the peoples that live along these shores: the many tribes of Bedouins, the Israelis and Jordanians to the north, and to the south the Egyptians, Saudis, Sudanese and Yemenites.

★ ★ ★

Later that day we arrived at our destination. It was the first time I had ever visited Nuweiba el Muzeina. There, the desert makes a quiet approach to the sea, a gentle slope. Its hills subside like a camel lying down, merge gently into beach, and dive into the waves. But the Red Sea does mark a scene of geological violence now softened by time, the course of the Great Rift Valley.

I did not then know this preserve of the Muzeini tribe. It is slightly off the beaten track, and its unexceptional beach did not draw visits until recently. Asher pointed out the tarmac road that runs to the sea's edge. Around us, a jumble of Bedouin tents, and concrete houses with patios and grazing donkeys, alternated with wide open sandy wastes, with not so much as a shrub. Small shops with painted signs displayed advertisements for Coca-Cola and alcohol-free beer. Their inscriptions in Arabic often accompanied the picture of a grinning dolphin.

The village sprawls along the coast. Facing the Red Sea, with its back to the sacred mountains of the Sinai, it is bathed in a heavenly light. It seemed to be booming. The low concrete walls were brand-new, patient dromedaries stood guard, and plump goats cavorted by the roadside. And dozens of children, their faces already beaten by the scorching sun, with bright clothes, barefoot or in battered sandals, ran around showing off their games and beaming smiles to visitors. Men whose forms were swollen by their jellabas, loose robes of spotless fine cotton, and women with supple walks and often a platter, a bundle of twigs or a pile of clothes balanced on their heads, greeted us with an easy wave. I smelled the familiar blend of charcoal, sea spray and sand as another sign of welcome. I was happy, already captured by the fullness of this corner of the world. It has never disappointed me.

We drove on past hand-painted signs with arrows pointing to DOLPHIN BEACH. ABID'ALLAH WELCOME!, they also declared. I was thinking that we would stay around there, but Asher wanted us to stay nearer the beach where Muhammad *el-atrach*, Deaf Muhammad, Abid'allah's best friend lived. Asher explained: 'You won't find better hospitality, and Abid'allah is always hanging out at Muhammad's place. Not to mention that he has the patience Abid'allah doesn't always manage, to tell stories about the past!'

At the entrance to the car park, some old men sitting in the shade asked whether I'd be staying or not, so as to know how much to charge. I called out through the open car window: 'I'm staying for a few days, *inshallah.*' Then they saw Asher and stood up. They embraced at length, with a simple: 'Asher! Asher! *Ahlan ou sahlan alikoum!* Welcome to you both!' They were visibly delighted to see each other. I too got out, escorted by a band of cheerful children. They clustered round, surprised and impressed by the stuff I was unloading from the car: my wheelchair and the rucksacks I attach to it.

I've never been without my wheelchair since 13 December 1984. It happened in

13

France. I was just seventeen, and studying for the baccalaureate. In the coldest winter of the decade, I was on my way to school, and just as the train was starting I slipped on a patch of ice below the next-to-last carriage and was sucked down by the in-draught. My whole body was dragged beneath the thundering train. When the alarm stopped it, fifty metres further on, I was lying between the rails and my legs were gone, mangled from the thighs downwards. My height was reduced from one metre sixty-five centimetres to exactly a metre: I now measure the distance between two rails of the French railway gauge. So now I travel in a wheelchair. It weighs eight kilos, I weigh forty-one, and between us we make a good team. Since then, I have looked at the world from the height of a ten-year-old, which offers me a particular eye-level view of our beautiful planet, and the undivided attention of children whose own height I measure up to.

★   ★   ★

I announced myself with a smile. Asher introduced me to our hosts, speaking clearly and making broad gestures. Muhammad nodded agreement, and without really looking at me gestured to his carpets, spread on

14

the ground just above the damp pebbles of the beach, by way of an invitation to join him. Everyone sat down; I know the Sinai ritual well. Words are no use. Looks and attitude make the first contacts, set the first mood, and perform the first exchanges. Most of all, the culture communicates through silence.

After some long peaceful minutes Muhammad tilted his head slightly and met my eye. This was the signal to start the introductions. The first smiles appeared. My first thought: 'He's really endearing, so shy and proud at the same time.' Serious people always amuse me, it must be opposites attracting.

He pointed to his lips and ears, and signalled 'out of order'. I smiled back. I already knew from Asher that he was deaf. It is a genetic deficiency of the Muzeini tribe and one in seven of the children born to the tribe are deaf. That's how it is — 'Allah gives and Allah takes away,' these Bedouins say. Later I prayed that He never takes away the joy in life and generosity of the Suleimans, the Atwas, and the other families of Muzeina.

I showed him my hands to signify: 'We'll talk in gestures, that'll do fine.' He seemed pleased with my attitude, and stood up. For my first lesson in this local sign language, he made some big gestures to ask me: 'Coffee or tea?'

He simplifies the sign language for strangers, so it's become a kind of universal sign Esperanto. 'Sugar?' he asked. 'How much?' I improvised, and asked around in Arabic for information about the other basic gestures that will enable us to start a conversation.

★ ★ ★

Below us, past the strip of pebbles that serves as a beach, and the foam, and a few metres of sea, I caught sight of the edge of the reef. The water there is clearer and forms sinuous opal shimmers. And there my gaze stopped: there she was. Olin was parading her fin, and sometimes the tip of a curious nose.

As if reading my mind my neighbour, a very frail young man with a slightly drooping left eye, informed me in sign language: 'She's always there.' I learned later that this is Juma, and he is Abid'allah's other boyhood friend. To differentiate him from the others, they call him 'the one-eyed deaf man', which he detests. He prefers to be called by his family name, which is signed by touching his right fist to his forehead.

He gave me a comical wide-eyed stare. 'Can you swim?' I looked back in amazement. 'Of course I can!' Stung by the question, I added idiotically: 'I was a member of the national swimming team in Israel, and I've won a few competitions ... ' Okay, I was boasting, but it's the truth. To prove it, I mimed in the air the crawl, breast-stroke, butterfly, and scuba diving. Juma had not understood what I had told him, and went off to find a boy who understood and spoke Hebrew. He took a few seconds to give a signed translation, which staggered me. In front of Juma, who seemed to be listening, I asked: 'Do all of you speak sign language?'

'Of course!' he replied with a grin. 'For us it's like Arabic, we learn it very young.'

What a lesson! The first of many in this simple, touching place. Many writers have described real or mythical worlds where a whole race has a physical feature that distinguishes it from the rest and enables it to develop special abilities. None of them has dared, I think, to imagine a land where men born different understand each other and live together, in the same way. Yet this reality exists: all the members of the Muzeini tribe, the hearers and the deaf, women and men, the young and the very old, can 'sign'. They all speak their sign language. I say 'their' because if you speak a Western sign language it is very hard at first to understand what they are saying: it is very much a dialect of their own, made up of gestures commonly used in the Near East — where people often speak with their hands — and signs accumulated over the years, some of them using the Arabic alphabet. Their language evolves every day: they have recently worked out signs that refer to every European nationality.

★ ★ ★

While this exchange was going on, Juma set about lining up a row of small coloured cushions, one after the other, from my seat to the edge of the water. Sitting on Muhammad's carpets, lovingly arranged in a quincunx, I remained speechless. I wasn't sure if I'd quite understood. Juma indicated in staccato sign language, articulating every gesture: 'Your wheelchair won't work on the beach. If you want to go swimming with Olin, you won't get hurt on the pebbles, you can hop from one cushion to the next.' He was so considerate that tears came to my eyes, and I blushed, but the others didn't bat an eyelid; that's the way things are done here.

Finishing the coffee, I made my way down my red carpet — though hardly as red as I — to the sea. Olin seemed to be watching our courtesies from the end of the cushioned path. Dressed in my swimsuit, mask and snorkel, only a few paces away from these men covered from head to foot in their immaculate jellabas, I slid softly into the crystal water of the Red Sea. I felt slightly awkward about my dress, in this traditional Islamic land, but the Bedouins of the Sinai know very well that for us Westerners it is natural for girls to wear swimsuits, just as boys do. Why not? Their ethnological view of our customs is broad and understanding.

The water is not really sea as we know it in Europe — neither the Atlantic Ocean nor the Mediterranean. It is not sea, it is home. It is warm, and almost free of waves. Even a glance under the surface transports me elsewhere, into the deep-sea space I love so much, although in the inlet of Muzeina the depths are poor in comparison with the other reefs. There are a few corals, and some seaweed, but the flow of sediment from the river that drains here during the few spells of rain inhibits the development of the fragile flora that grows in beauty everywhere else along this magic coast.

* * *

I had returned to the sensations of this tropical sea. It lives in my dreams when I am far away, caught in an overcast Paris or a restless Jerusalem. But what's more, Olin is here. I couldn't quite see her yet, but I could hear her. She was circling somewhere outside my field of vision, and inspecting me with her sonar. I heard that very special sound that resembles a shrill decoding machine, a faint noise of changing frequency occupying all the undersea space around me. I took it as a signal of welcome and swam slowly, feeling her presence.

Then she appeared. She was majestic. Her sheer bulk, which I had not reckoned on, loomed towards me. Olin measures two metres ten centimetres long, and must weigh something like two hundred kilos. She moved through the sea as if by levitation, glided without moving, as if by some unknown spiritual force. With a sharp and almost brutal surge, she speeded up and vanished into the blue, which looked utterly dark. I became quickly aware of who she is. She is truly the master of this stretch of beach and of all its outer depths. She was arresting, and immense. The dolphin is definitely no kind of domestic animal, so it may seem odd to say it, but her wildness stuck out a mile. It needed this space, it clothed her in such dignity.

Soon after she came back and stayed put, three or four metres away from me. She scanned me again with her internal radar, her power of echolocation, which enables her to pinpoint objects or people and build a mental image of them without seeing them: she already knew how I am built better than I do myself. She waited for my response. I stayed passive and swam quietly, with my hands folded behind me to indicate acknowledgement: I was in her world, and my human character conferred no rights over her.

The message of the books that I consulted before I came was that dolphins are particularly sensitive to body language, so I was trying to put this into practice. Olin didn't come any closer, though, but circled me, at different depths, taking my measure. I called to her under the water through my snorkel, reciting 'Olin, Olin . . . ' like a mantra.

She began to move imperceptibly closer with every turn; soon she was only a metre and a half away. As I wasn't moving, the water was starting to chill me to the bone. I decided to join my new Bedouin hosts in the shade of the palm-tree-leaf awning. I turned, showing Olin that I was returning to the beach.

She followed, brushing me gently and skimming my right side with the whole of her supple body before she too turned away. 'Bye-bye, pal,' I answered in my mind.

Muhammad was waiting, squatting on the pebbles with two bottles of fresh water at his feet and a terry towel over his arm. When I emerged from the water he poured three litres of warm water over my head. What bliss! As it trickled down my body, it washed off the roughness of the sea salt. I dried myself, and put my clothes back on for a soft return over the gaudy cushions. Feeling like a queen frog on her lily pads, I intercepted some of the glances aimed towards me, but they were not elusive, or pitying, or bemused, and lacked even the natural curiosity about an unusual sight. I believe that the Bedouins were looking at me the way I look at myself, over ten years after the accident. Where do they draw that power from?

They waited impatiently. 'So, what happened with Olin?' They had been watching our performance from the beach, and didn't miss her last goodbye when I came out. I told the story. Salem explained in Hebrew: 'We thought she would notice your handicap and come closer to you than to someone she doesn't know.' I commented out loud: 'I don't think so. She noticed my size, but I swim like everybody else, I don't think I'm anything special for her.' Silence fell again.

Little by little, Olin's magic was settling inside me. I resolved to come back to swim with her that evening.

★   ★   ★

On the beach there was life everywhere. The little girls were distributing their pretty smiles and deftly woven bright cotton bracelets to passers-by, for three Egyptian pounds, forty-five pence. Muhammad's neighbours, all of them men, sat by to listen to the latest talk. Each of them spoke as he pleased, and left as he came. That is the way news travels in Muzeina. Clinton's confessions, Arafat's illness, and the fame of the international football star Zidane of Marseille have reached this far. They even asked me whether Zinedine Zidane is not an Arab too, or maybe a Berber, and whether it would be right to include him with pride in the praises of local heroes. I knew that the information sifted between them would become common knowledge in the village. But nobody asked me who I was. They could certainly see that I had come from Tel Aviv, because they knew at a glance my number plate, my Arabic accent, and my type of colouring. And above all they had all known Asher for such a long time . . . my friendship with him was a first-class passport.

But the first, the one and only, personal question didn't take too long to come. 'Are you married? Have you got children?' This was decisive for defining my person and status among the Bedouins. Disinclined to explain my European view of cohabiting, I did as I usually do on my travels: I lied. 'Yes, married quite recently. *Inshallah*, we will have children . . . ' They admired my courage as a lone woman who travels long distances.

The sky was magnificent and the sea gleamed like a jewel of layered blues in its casket of reef, sand, and sparkling pebbles. I openly took out my first small notebook and an old Bic and started to write.

*   *   *

For several days I waited on the beach in order to meet Abid'allah, listening to various people's stories, breathing in the rich air of this magical place, and trying to understand what makes it so. When he finally returned to the village from his fishing trip one of the village boys, little Ramadan, came running to let me know: 'He's gone to swim with Olin. As soon as he's out, I'll take you to him!' The intuition and kindness shown by Bedouins to their guests is legendary, but sometimes it

24

catches you by surprise. Especially when it comes from an urchin barely ten years old.

I could already see Abid'allah in the distance. I knew that it was him. Wet through, and coated with sea salt, but wreathed in a huge smile with perfect teeth, he was a good-looking boy. I greeted him in the local sign language. This really surprised him, made him beam even more, hurrying towards me and hugging me as if he had known me for ever.

He spoke in an odd guttural Hebrew. 'Hey! *Ma nichma*? What's new?' I burst out laughing. I too had the strong impression that I knew him. If he was aware that I had made it my business to read and hear all that had been said about him . . . in fact, I believe that he sensed at once that I knew him a little already, and must have been flattered or amused; it was as if he read my intentions in seconds, with no interpreter or dictionary. He adopted me from that moment we met.

He laughed again. 'I swam a long way out with Olin, to find some peace and quiet. We hadn't seen each other for several days, the two of us. We went out playing under water, found a sea cucumber and played ball.' I wonder if he's joshing or if he's simply reporting an everyday fact. 'She loves to play,' Muhammad confirmed. Abid'allah cut in:

'Hey! Will you come swimming with me tomorrow?' I accepted without a moment's hesitation — I wanted to see them together under water, to learn about their exceptional relationship. What makes it work? I tried the question on Abid'allah, and he laughed fit to burst — a laugh of contentment, it seems, and one of pride that I recognize his treasure. 'She loves me and I love her!' I thought as much. Questions are not his thing.

★ ★ ★

Abid'allah woke me gently from where I had been sleeping in the open, on the beach. I'd drifted off looking at a night sky so crowded with stars it was as if I was actually amongst them, and could reach out to touch them, and as though the Milky Way was stroking my hair. Abid'allah asked me, in words and gestures: 'Are you coming swimming with Olin?' I said yes, and slipped into my swimsuit inside my sleeping-bag. It was already warm, the timid sun seeping through and thinning the transparent haze, a few scattered diamond flashes dazzling me.

The beach was still asleep. I love that feeling of perfect calm, only the little birds in the palm trees starting to chirp with their long beaks, only the dew's evaporation reminding you that you are awake, even if the place is still motionless with night.

Abid'allah stood facing the sun, his feet washed by streamers of foam. Against the sunlight, his silhouette looked huge and edged with gold. We entered the cool water and together swam slowly towards the horizon. Dazzled, and not yet awake, I didn't notice Olin following us, just a few centimetres behind, although Abid'allah knew she was there all along. She nosed between us and grazed Abid'allah. I stroked the soft warm rubber skin of her smooth flank.

When I murmured 'Olin, Olin' underwater, she came a little closer, and I stroked her fin with my fingertips — dolphins enjoy that. We were getting to know each other, but I didn't want to overdo the touching; when she moved off I stayed still. She had sobered me up from my sleep. Her presence has infinite power.

And then with a flick of her tail she was standing upright in front of Abid'allah, to have her throat stroked, with her snout rising straight from the water. How could she hold that position without moving? Abid'allah trod water to stay where he was and petted her, crying her name and laughing out loud. What a moment! The scene was so joyful that it made me laugh too. Abid'allah shot a glance at me, delighting in our collusion.

Suddenly, as if at a soundless signal, they raced off in unison, almost belly to belly, facing each other. Their two bodies looped and crossed over, met and moved away, in a wonderful underwater dance. Between them they formed a great eye that gently opened and closed. I followed them some metres back, a stunned observer: the sea belonged to them. With Abid'allah, Olin will go far out to sea, whereas on her own she often lingers in her chosen zone of the lagoon. Their relationship is free and easy. They seem to understand each other body to body, like two lovers who have known each other for a long time.

Abid'allah gave Olin's back a vigorous stroking, while she bowed her head on to his shoulder. With her flippers, as if they were hands, she stroked his arms and ribs, and he clasped her nose for a kiss. I felt moved and almost embarrassed to be a spectator at such an intimate scene. Their bodies then formed an arrow, it seemed as if they were merging, the dolphin's body growing human, Abid'allah's becoming a dolphin's. I thought of those ancient images of Eros or Aphrodite, gods of love, breasting a wave astride a dolphin.

As they set off into the distance, I decided

not to go with them. Abid'allah beckoned me to follow, but I didn't want to. Those two loved each other, and I needed to get back to dry land. I was longing for a small cup of strong Arab coffee. When I reached the shore I found one waiting. Bliss.

★   ★   ★

I forgot Abid'allah the man for a whole day and night, instead taking the time to soak myself in everything I heard so as to understand the detail of his story. Every day in Muzeina I learn of different forms of communication between people, in languages and in sign language, but learn in particular that friendship itself is a language whose forms do not matter at all.

Each time I go swimming, I build a little on my relationship with Olin. Little by little we discover each other, though our body dialogue stumbles compared with my friends Abid'allah, Juma and Muhammad. Most of Olin's friends are deaf — perhaps their habit of gestural and physical language brings them closer. Yet certain children of the tribe also have a true contact with her that I will never have, or perhaps I would have to live here to achieve it.

Questions occur to me about the way that

dolphins relate among themselves. I wonder whether or not the bond between Olin and Abid'allah echoes a relationship she might have had with another dolphin. A different world is unfolding in front of me, posing thousands of questions and offering me a new passion. The friendships that dwell in this gulf have already caught me for good in their net.

★ ★ ★

Abid'allah went off fishing again for the rest of the week. One night as several of us sat talking with Muhammad by candle-light, the tea waiting in its ornate pot, Ahmed Suleiman, a cousin of Abid'allah, came to sit near us on the carpets. 'Do you know the story about Abid'allah when he was still small?' he signed to me. 'His family, the Mekhassens, and my family have been friends since the time of the Prophet ... ' I had already heard some childhood scraps, but not always mutually consistent. 'Tell me ... ' I signed to him.

I took out my already crumpled notebook and my pen, and put them down in front of me for all to see.

Abid'allah's story

Connected to the Arabian Desert, the mountains of the Sinai, carved by sea tides and furrowed by the centuries, protect the Red Sea as an oyster shell guards its precious pearl. Thanks to their sixty-one thousand square kilometres of rock, the khamsin, the terrible wind of the Arab deserts, does not reach this far; it stays with the Bedouins on the other side, who know it too well and bear it with sympathy, the way you listen to an old man repeating the same old stories. The sea is deep here — up to seventeen hundred metres — and carpeted with walls of tropical reefs, some of the most incredible in the world. It is the contrast between this azure blue and the vast desert reaches surrounding it that makes this place at once different and compelling. Allah created a wonder by joining extremes in harmony.

Tonight, the storm's dark fingers are scooping up waves of thick, oily indigo. The wind drives the howl of the sea towards the continent. It dumps its salt and tramples the heavy pebbles of the Nuweiba el Muzeina shoreline. Massive and steady, the glowing red rocks reach down and merge with it to bless it and to give it a name: the Red Sea.

* * *

In the tent of the Mekhassens, Abid'allah, their latest baby, is swaddled inside a big camel-hair burnous against a baptism of rain. His smile has faded: he fears the storm. His skin is honey, his eyes are honey, and he is frowning with all his might. He makes up his mind to cry.

His cousin Ahmed Suleiman arrives, his arms as wide open as his smile. Without a word he picks up the child and walks around cradling him. The tent, six woven goat-hair carpets each more than ten metres long, is tethered to the ground by hemp ropes. It briefly allows the year's first rain to seep inside like a light mist — ten minutes' homage to the life-saving water — then the hair swells up with moisture and proudly protects those inside all season long.

The brilliance in Ahmed's gaze is reflected in Abid'allah's, who also starts to chuckle: Ahmed sits the boy on his lap and makes deft gestures with his slender fingers, explaining the storm. Wordlessly, he draws circles, puffing his cheeks with the astounded eyes of a man faced with the power of nature. The wind — not the ordinary wind from the north, but the one that comes from the west and brings the cloud — is blowing today; it is winter for two months, and the rare rainfall is *wa'abel*: downpour and floods. Yet this the Bedouins pray to see and hear. Nomads, they travel from well to well, and oasis to oasis, as the seasons command, with their families and the few belongings that make up the household. Fresh water is life in the Sinai, as in all the world's deserts, and wells are vital organs — the Bedouins' eyes.

The water collected on the tent drains towards a small stone placed on the roof, gathers there, falls, and gushes down to feed into a bowl that forms a small spring in the corner of the tent. Outside Abid'allah hears the rustle of the heavy fabrics covering the body of Jamia, his young mother, and the familiar swish of her sandals through the sand.

He has jumped up to greet her. Only his sudden movement warns Ahmed that she is coming, because he himself has never heard the soft rustle of the Bedouin women's thick robes, nor any other sound.

★ ★ ★

This early in the winter, the heavy tents are still pitched near the sea, which teems with fish. The goats, donkeys and camels are busy harvesting the explosion of fragile vegetation. While his father is away, fishing with his big brothers and cousins, Abid'allah is at a loose end, fidgeting round his mother like a spinning top run wild. Always on the move, he tries to climb the walls of the house and turn them into a makeshift toboggan slope. Never stopping for breath, he entices his pals in the tribe into funny games. They dig imaginary wells and fill them with water from gourds that quickly run dry — the litres of water drawn by patient women a kilometre away, wasted in an instant by these excited kids . . . Jamia is furious: the threshold of her tent looks like a network of muddy trenches. Her son takes his smack with a grin — he doesn't seem to know what anger is.

Ever since he first strung childish words together, Abid'allah has told endless imaginary tales that the grownups don't understand and which worry his mother. He is just four years old when his hyperactive moods take Jamia to visit Umm Fatma, the *dotora*, the village healer who knows the traditional Bedouin herbs and medicines. She also sees things, and her advice is as precious as life.

'Jamia, this child is possessed, he must be

protected. Something is going to happen to him, to do with the sea.' Umm Fatma heaves a long sigh and frowns. She lays a hand on the boy's chest, and for once he doesn't dare to move. 'Jamia, my girl, take him away from the sea.' Her solemn, visionary tone leaves no room for doubt or questions. But Bedouins do not normally take their children near the water anyway. Umm Fatma's face is transformed, marked with pent-up terror. 'Try not to keep him too close to yourself.'

The verdict fell like a sharpened knife on a chicken's neck. The *dotora* must have noticed that Abid'allah is my favourite son, thinks Jamia . . . but she feels I mustn't get too fond of him — why not? Because his life will be short? In tears, Jamia goes home and hides in her tent. It isn't good to show weakness in front of others, so she waits, numbly, for her husband or the night to return.

★   ★   ★

Even before the early morning mist, Jamia goes out to prepare the big flat round pancakes that will be the staple food for the journey. She has made up her mind overnight: she wants to remove her son from the beach and return as soon as possible to the mountains. She first gathers dried twigs.

Her fire takes the place of the russet moon and drives away the dark till the following night. On to the rounded griddle she throws the heavy dough that flattens and crackles. The rich aroma of hot bread is starting to waft around the tent when her husband appears, back from his fishing voyage, a camel's rein in one hand and a basketful of fish in the other, looking fatigued. She welcomes him with tea, lovingly sweetened, and starts to clean the fish. 'Jamia, a Bedouin mustn't stay long in the same place. We leave for the mountains tomorrow,' he says, before she can tell him anything of her own feelings.

Jamia takes this as an omen: her husband, who does not know about the *dotora*'s prediction, has sensed that they ought to leave. The message is clear: to protect Abid'allah, they must take him away from the sea. They will go back to the desert around Bir Zrir, Arabic for 'Little Well', where, next to the region's best source of fresh water, she often spent time with her mother, till the day of her marriage at fifteen.

They have the nomad's departure to prepare. Dismantling and folding the goat-hair tent, coiling the ropes, collecting the kitchen utensils and packing the few clothes. And in particular, rounding up the livestock. Their entire wealth is their herd of goats and dromedaries, from which they derive milk, meat, wool for the tent and some of their clothes. They move either on foot or on camel-back.

After the meal, Abid'allah's father wants to take him to the beach at Nuweiba el Muzeina to tend the date palms. The delighted Abid'allah puts on a small jellaba over his shorts and takes his father's hand. Jamia is afraid: 'Take care of him, and see that he doesn't go near the water!'

Each family of the Muzeini tribe has its own date palms on this beach. Territorial boundaries are determined by the trees, which every father bequeaths to his first-born son. Admiringly, Abid'allah watches his father scale them using the rough bulges on their hairy flaking stems. They often measure four to six metres tall, and in winter the heavy bunches of dates have to be insulated from the cold by wrappings of cloth or plastic bags. In Arabic, as in Hebrew, each part and branch of the palm tree has a specific name; this tree is a precious resource in the region. Like the camel, it seems to have been imported from what is now Iraq, perhaps four thousand years ago.

Abid'allah's neck aches from watching his father up among the crowns. He starts to dream that he too is big, and climbing date palms to help his father. But soon the work is over, and the fruits protected till harvest time. It is time to go home and make ready the camels, theirs and their Suleiman cousins', that will be leaving with them.

★   ★   ★

Dawn next day finds Abid'allah and his brother Eid perched on the tent, itself stowed on top of the utensils and water gourds, skilfully arranged around the camel's tall leather saddle. Jamia and her husband walk beside them, followed by the Suleiman family and three meharis — riding dromedaries. Without looking back at the sea, they leave the coast by a gently sloping sandy road, and then by the steep pathways that wind across the pink granite landscape up to villages high in the heart of the Sinai mountains.

Four days of marching follow, with long waits in the shade of nooks in the rocks till the heat subsides. The gait of the camels seems fragile, their ankles so slim, and with every step their plodding hoofs seem heavier, yet they go on, stolid and surely slightly stupid too. Before long Abid'allah is hopping with impatience on top of the towering beast, telling his spellbound elder brother wild tales about djinns, evil spirits best avoided, and sirens, all invented as they go along.

Their train follows the folds of ridges creased by sea and time. Now and again it encounters the sort of wild beauty that seems as if it has escaped from the pages of a Japanese print book, and the malice of angry, scowling outcropping rocks. At their feet they find occasional flat white limestone trails, punctuated by sharp and sturdy young acacia, or by a *radjum*, a cairn of three big stones that serves as a desert signal, possibly left by Abid'allah's grandfather. Whether it marks a battle in the past, or announces a water hole, it greets whoever passes by.

We all have a *radjum* of some sort in the back of our minds, a dream of the desert. In the West, we see the desert as the ultimate symbol of emptiness and solitude. We speak about 'crossing the wilderness' for a period of unwanted isolation, or 'a voice in the wilderness' for speaking without being heard. We have forgotten the basic meaning in the Bible, where the root of the word desert, *midbar*, means 'word' in Hebrew. The Sinai desert is word, divine and human, whose echoes from mountain to mountain bind people together. There, everything is known, thanks to the rumours that speed from well to well, from caravan to caravan, from *radjum* to signs. The whole population of the desert has access, at its ancestral tempo, to news from all over the world.

The Ten Commandments, in Hebrew the ten words, seem to have been given to Moses in these bare mountains, the place where he led the people of Israel out of their time of slavery, the place where he made them cross over the Red Sea so as to reach the Promised Land. And all the prophets, Christian, Muslim and Jewish, have found their inspiration and their word in the desert — often this very desert, the Sinai.

For wisdom is spoken in this place, which belongs both to no one in particular, and to any who venture into it.

Feiran oasis, winter 1979

In order to enjoy the lush spring of Ain Houdra, after crossing the Baraka, the giant sea of white sand, Abid'allah's family caravan travels past the imposing outer wall of St Catherine's monastery, which since its building in the Middle Ages has always housed a dozen Orthodox Christian monks. It is guarded traditionally by the Gabaliyya tribe, who number about fifteen hundred today, some of them with mad blue eyes, the descendants of stevedores from the Black Sea coast dispatched by the Emperor Justinian in 532, to serve the monks.

Jamia and her husband have never been inside the grounds. The thought doesn't enter their minds, even though this place is as holy for Muslims as it is for Jews and Christians. Bedouins are people of the desert, and believe first of all in the absolute immanence of Allah: to be shut inside walls, and protected from the desert so as to pray, is not for them. Yet behind its low, wide, studded metal doors, narrow paved paths with whitewashed walls are laden with bougainvillaea and glossy plants. Although in the open desert, and under the same sun, the genius of these men of faith has protected each stone with another one, each stretch of path with a green and silver olive tree. Everything thrives here, and is cool.

The Mekhassens skirt Mount Jabel Thuna, enter the pass of El-Boueid, and reach the well of the Feiran oasis where the winter tents left behind months ago, hanging from the acacia trees, wait for them like faithful guardians. The Bedouins of the Sinai always leave some of their belongings in the open desert: their tents, clothing, or even treasures hidden in small caves signposted by a *radjum*. Nobody touches them: that is the custom, the law of the tribes. The mutual trust of the Bedouins never fails.

With the same devotion to duty that they showed long ago, in the days of the caravans that carried spices, fabrics or salt from one continent to the other, the camels drink nothing but brackish water that humans cannot stomach. On the other hand, they get to drink first. The few gourds and vessels left there have absorbed the dust and winds, but the two young women prepare tea for the long stopover; after such a march, hot drinks are more advisable.

Bir Zrir village, spring 1980

Abid'allah is jumping from Ahmed's lap on to that of Ahmed's younger brother Darwish, also born deaf. He won't let them make the fire for dinner, and his father gets cross.

After camp has been pitched, Darwish tells his parents that he wants to marry Fatma, the *dotora*'s daughter. The moment seems right. His father rounds up a fat sheep to endear him to his intended's family, and goes looking for the sheikh who will oversee the exchanges, as tradition demands. This ceremony, the *jaha*, does not permit the girl's name to be spoken; only those of the families possibly soon to be united are mentioned.

The *dotora* is outside the tent, breastfeeding her latest daughter, her breast only just hidden by the black crêpe veil that swathes her hair and lower face. Her eyes light up at the sight of her guests arriving with the *mansaf*, a big copper tray, loaded with food, balanced on Darwish's mother's head: she understands their purpose straight away, and already knows that she consents, but her daughter Fatma huddles in the tent and weeps. She is ready to marry, but someone she can love. '*Ummi*, he's deaf, I won't be able to live with him. How would he speak to me? How would he speak to his children?' The anxious mother takes her in her arms. 'You'll speak to him in sign language, like everybody else. Let's see what your coffee grounds say. Then you will make your choice.' Fatma agrees to listen to the omens.

With one deft gesture, the *dotora* up-ends her glass over a white saucer. Attentively she scans the patterns drawn by the coffee grains swirled on to the rim of the glass drunk by the girl. 'You see that curve, daughter, pointing at the glass's inner edge? It stands for serenity. It is a happy future, fond love, and fine healthy children.' Fatma doesn't speak, and the *dotora* tries to reassure her. 'Fatma, what you choose is right. Do as your heart directs you, it is as pure as spring water.' The girl is troubled; the omens are favourable. She is also reluctant to wait for some new suitor ... She decides to go and ask advice from Jamia, her cousin and great friend. Her answer is clear: the young deaf man is the right sort. His family too. The Suleimans come from ancient stock in Nuweiba el Muzeina. A few days later, Fatma agrees to marry Darwish.

★ ★ ★

For Bedouins, a house is a woman's place, because everything belongs to her, it is the husband's dowry, his wedding gift, equipped for every necessity in the daily life of the couple and their children to be. Fatma receives all this and a pair of solid gold bracelets from Darwish's parents, whose son's smile is brighter since that day. He is nineteen, she is fifteen. The feast is grand: several sheep and even a camel are slaughtered, the fare is delicious. In the morning the dancing gives way to storytelling and to serious conversation. Little Abid'allah doesn't remember his friend Darwish's wedding: he sleeps on the ground by the fire, a little bit tipsy with excitement.

Next morning everyone is glad, and Fatma seems happy with her marriage feast and her choice. As for Darwish, the tribe can't help teasing him: 'Keep smiling like that and your teeth will fall out. Shut your mouth once in a while.' In the afternoon torpor the women go to the well to draw water, but in particular to chat among themselves with no children in attendance and no pricked masculine ears. 'The wedding was a great success,' Jamia begins. Her cousin goes on: 'The *dotora* saw that the deaf boy is good for her daughter . . . She's right. He's resourceful, he's very nice — I wouldn't have said no!' The cousin's woeful tone causes chuckles: all the women are well aware that she doesn't get on with her husband. She heaves a sigh. 'He's such a fool, my man . . . I could leave him down the well . . . ' They all burst out laughing good-naturedly . . . of course it's no joke, but there's nothing to be done. There is no divorce among the nomads. The men can disown, and the women have a sense of humour. The politeness of despair, as a Yiddish saying goes.

* * *

The weeks slip by round the big tents scattered through the nomad's camp. The Mekhassens', the Suleimans', and the newly-weds' tent, lent to them till they come to a mountain village where a new one can be made and sewn together.

Fatma and Jamia have left for a nearby wadi, looking for some medicinal herbs requested by the *dotora*, who is teaching her daughter everything she knows. The camels from each herd graze free, wherever the dunes and contours of this arid land allow them to roam. You can hear their braying chime with the trowels of the men who work to shore up the little sandy irrigated terraces where vegetables grow in the shade of date palms and fig trees.

Bir Zrir, summer 1980

Someone comes running. It's Darwish, and he is waving his arms in the distance. There's something wrong . . . 'Allah! Allah!' the women are crying already, to ward off ill fortune. Too late. Darwish signals the height of a child of five, and revolves his arms on each side of his chest like a locomotive . . . 'Abid'allah!' his mother screams. 'Something bad has happened to him . . . ' she whispers voicelessly, before singing into the arms of her stunned cousin.

Blood, plum-coloured blood, trickles from both of Abid'allah's small ears. He doesn't cry, but his face is nothing but a scrap of damp cloth wrung with pain. Though he does not appear to be breathing, he is panting softly so as to avoid any movement. He is lying at the foot of one of the oasis date palms, below the big branch that he fell from, pinned like a butterfly in a display case.

Ahmed is holding his hand. 'Little Abid'allah, what's happening to you?' say his eyes. Abid'allah's father arrives at a run, scoops him up from the ground and heads off. Ahmed is frozen. What can he do by himself, and on foot? He too goes racing off, to Sheikh Ramadan's tent, a kilometre distant, to borrow his Jeep. He drives to catch up with Mekhassen, who is still frantically running. He must be heading for the hospital at Nuweiba, ten kilometres away.

You can't mistake their little cloud of dust. Ahmed brakes and opens the passenger door for them, and they make for the Israeli hospital. Abid'allah has fainted with the pain; his father is shuddering with fear. Ahmed drives fast and well — he works on the John Deere, the big tractor at Asher's melon moshav in Nuweiba. Spotted from a window in the distance, the speeding Jeep alerts the casualty department to expect the worst. After several minutes' examination, the verdict is harsh: both eardrums are burst, the inner ears crushed, there is cranial trauma, and the risk of an aneurysm. The doctors are utterly clear: his only chance is to take him straight to the regional hospital in Elat. Abid'allah is nodding his head and wheezing alarmingly . . . But they must also *pay* for the transport and medical care . . . Ahmed and Mekhassen exchange bewildered glances. Ahmed signs Asher's name, Mekhassen assents and speaks in halting Hebrew: 'We have Israeli employers, they'll see to everything with their insurance . . . ' They know nothing about it of course, but it is the only chance left for Abid'allah, reduced to a shallow breath, unconscious between the white sheets, his head now streaked with clotted blood and bandages. The doctors decide to turn a blind eye to standard procedure about payment: five years old is no age to die, even in some far corner of the Sinai. Everything speeds up, and Abid'allah and his father are ferried by helicopter to the modern hospital complex. The scanner and exhaustive tests show that there is no point in opening the skull. The ENT surgeon examines and cleans the sleeping child's ears. The diagnosis comes. He will live, but the after-effects are serious. He may well be permanently deaf.

Ahmed does not waste any time. Leaving the
Jeep on the beach at Muzeina when it runs
out of fuel, he sets off again to tell the whole
story to the Israeli employer, because all this
may cost the tribe very dear . . . He takes his
bicycle, and covers the four kilometres from
the beach to the moshav with his jellaba
hitched above his knees. Asher Gal, an
athletic, dour little man with small round
glasses and bushy eyebrows (which is just
how the deaf of Muzeina sign him, miming
the two thick arches), is busy doing what he
loathes most of all: entertaining his accountant. Glad of an excuse to escape, the Israeli
jumps to his feet and sticks his hand out, then
peers in surprise at his visitor. 'Your smile is
so sad today,' he mimes in improvised sign
language. 'What's the matter?' Ahmed,
relieved to be asked questions, squats
cross-legged on the ground, inviting his less
supple host to do the same. He embarks on
the story with slow gestures, repeating the
most important sections. Asher repeats aloud
in Hebrew what he understands his friend is
saying. 'The little Mekhassen boy, the cheeky
one . . . yes, I know him . . . a fall from a date
palm. Almost died . . . the Bedouins in a
panic . . . Then what? What happened after

the accident?' Ahmed hesitates. Asher shakes his arm. 'Come on!'

'We took him to the clinic at Nuweiba, but it was no good . . . the doctors sent him to Elat.'

Ahmed feels he has said it all, but Asher is still at a loss, and asks again: 'How is the boy?'

'More or less all right, he'll live, but he's going to be deaf,' says the Bedouin.

'Deaf?' Asher is thunderstruck. Deaf by accident, in this tribe where so many are deaf by birth, through congenital defects. 'It's almost unbelievable,' he murmurs. Ahmed looks him straight in the eyes and waits. 'Is there something I can do?' Asher adds shrewdly, knowing his employee well. Ahmed nods assent, feeling both pleased and nervous. 'The hospital,' he mimes, 'is very, very, very expensive. Can they' — he points northward and signs with two fingers on one shoulder, the authorities: by 'them' he means Israel, the government, the insurance companies, the official ones or some specialist department — 'can they pay?'

Asher turns slightly pale. On the chair behind him, the accountant clears his throat impatiently. 'OK, Asher, let's finish here and then I'll let you go. What's he saying, to get you so worked up?'

50

'Nothing, I've got to find a few thousand dollars to pay hospital fees for the Mekhassen boy.'

'How much?'

'Well, nobody knows! A lot, that's for sure, he's bound to be in surgery ... well, it's better than a grave ... but where is the cash going to come from?'

Asher mutters to himself, and Ahmed thanks him, forgetting to mention the helicopter trip, and walks away, convinced that his boss will help.

'Hey!' Asher grabs him by the arm. 'I'm not yet *sure* I can sort this out. Come back tomorrow.'

Ahmed promises, then goes off, feeling relieved.

'Just great!' his boss grumbles. 'We'd have to apply to the insurance people to pay off on a working accident, but who's going to believe in a worker who's only five years old!'

'Unless they forget to mention it,' the accountant remarks blandly.

'Yeah, right, are you nuts? A proper accountant, you don't know these doctors. Also, in Elat they think they're God almighty, like all provincial bigshots!'

'I do, as it happens. Know them, I mean. The surgeon who thinks he's God is my brother Eli,' says the accountant, doing his best not to laugh.

'You're kidding me,' Asher flares.

'No, Mister Eyebrows, Eli Hirschman is my eldest brother, he's been in the paediatric department there for getting on for ten years.'

'He's the kid's doctor?'

'We'll soon find out.' Hirschman the accountant taps out his brother's number on the phone. 'Eli, hello, it's Rafuz. Listen, have you had a Bedouin boy arrive today, five years old, damaged ears? Really messed up? Yeah, now listen, he's the son of my client's employee, a farmer in the Nuweiba moshav, flat broke, need I say. We're putting the father's name down to get the insurance. OK? I'm relying on you. My client's name is Asher Gal, the one from the moshav, a grouch but all right. Thanks . . . Yes, 'bye! That's it,' he says, and hangs up. 'Now, help me get your bills sorted out, OK?'

* * *

Ahmed returns to the village. People flock round, but he makes straight for Jamia's tent, without a gesture. Fatma is there, sharing the endless wait with the mother praying for her son. 'Give thanks to Allah, Abid'allah lives,' he signs. She breaks down in tears of relief, and throws her arms around Ahmed, her entire posture thanking him for what he has done.

52

Fatma brings him *maramiya*, sweet sage tea, and he gives his recital of the fall, the journey, the hospital, good fortune, technology, the miracle . . . He leaves out the coma, the doctors' worried faces, the blood, the fear, and the hospital expenses. In particular, he leaves out the final diagnosis: the boy has lost all hearing in his right ear, and all but thirty per cent in his left ear.

⋆　⋆　⋆

From that day on, the minds of the Muzeini are permanently impressed by the life-saving Western technology and organization, but even more by enormous gratitude towards Asher Gal of the moshav.

The next week Mekhassen, followed by all the other Bedouin employees, comes to the moshav to convey his formal thanks to Asher and to invite him, as custom demands, to three days and nights of celebrations in his honour. Asher is visibly touched and embarrassed. Is it because he knows that the Mekhassens can't really afford such extravagance? He thinks it over, and finally he says: 'Do you know what my three children dream about?' No one has any idea. 'They dream of going off into the desert on camel-back, the way your children do.' Everyone is amazed.

'Could you come with us by camel to Bir Zrir and back, say in three days' time?' Mekhassen grins from ear to ear. 'When do you want to start?'

The deal is done: the feast becomes a simple friendly evening round the fire, and the trip is set for two weeks' time, during the school holidays. Everyone feels glad, and Asher's children most of all. Twenty years on, they still remember.

The swimming lesson

Nuweiba el Muzeina beach, summer 1981

Abid'allah no longer hears, no longer speaks. He doesn't say a word, and ignores his young neighbours, his former friends. He wanders by himself among the tents. Against the prognosis, the accident has left him stone deaf. Sad weeks drag by, and when Jamia is not at the well the gossip is painful to hear: 'The little mite has had it. He was already highly strung before the accident, and this is the end.' Fatma goes on: 'He must be under a spell. Maybe Allah is punishing the Mekhassens for some wrong done in the past . . . The grandfather's eldest was a rogue. He made both his wives suffer a lot.' The cousin sighs. 'Poor Jamia, it's not her fault. It's lucky she has her first boy. Eid is already going to school, he's very clever. That will save her. All the same . . . '

Jamia is expecting a third child. She keeps watch on Abid'allah to keep him from leaving their tent.

★   ★   ★

'Until you teach him how to swim, I won't let him go outside. You've got to promise me . . . ' Jamia keeps repeating, with more and more urgent gestures. Ahmed does not understand, though he does see that since their return to the coast Jamia has been closer than ever to her son, and on the alert. She clearly has an obsession, often describing a nightmare: Abid'allah runs off into the sea, and suffers a new disaster . . .

Yet with all his natural empathy, Ahmed reacts: 'Why would I teach him to swim? In the mountains, there's no point being able to swim anyway . . . Most of us can't, and so what?' This time he leaves with a dismissive gesture, then clasps both hands to his chest and repeats: '*Nissa, nissa* . . . women, women . . . '

An hour later, Darwish, the young husband, comes up behind the Mekhassen tent and shuffles his feet ostentatiously, so as to be invited inside. This is the tradition: to be asked to come in, you have to announce yourself by enacting a halt. He greets Jamia, and volunteers to take the former little devil under his wing. 'Yes, and to teach Abid'allah to swim . . . ' He smiles, happy to do his good deed for the day. 'Now? All right, now,' he nods, unable to resist Jamia's will.

At six years old Abid'allah has never set

foot in the sea. Darwish holds his pupil safe against his spotless jellaba, which is hitched up to his knees. He lays him flat on the water, and walks along the reef, which is not deep. The boy doesn't move. The sea is like the desert: all beginnings and no end. Darwish pats the water next to him and splashes him gently, to give him the idea ... Then something happens that no one has seen for a while: Abid'allah starts laughing. He no longer feels afraid. His cousin joins in.

They venture a little further out. With his free foot and arm, Darwish mimes the breaststroke and invites Abid'allah to do the same. Darwish is no longer standing on the edge of the reef. Suddenly Abid'allah up-ends himself and arrows headlong down into the deep water. The novice teacher can't move a muscle, stiff with shock and fear. Umm Fatma's prophecy is coming true before his very eyes! As bubbles boil up to the surface, Darwish plunges beneath them. He manages to grab the boy's arm and haul him back up, red in the face and spouting water. Panting for breath, Darwish resolves he will never tell Jamia what has happened ... But Abid'allah will have to understand the facts of the sea, learn how to swim ... Allah preserve him!

Very early next morning, Darwish collects Abid'allah from his mother for his second lesson. Muhammad and Juma, both six years old, and both of them deaf from birth, are already waiting for the novice instructor, sitting on the beach. They sign to him: 'Is it true you're teaching Abid'allah to swim? We want to too.' Darwish almost collapses. He'll never make it. With only one of them — admittedly the worst — it was mission impossible. With three ... he is already imagining the three little blue bodies washed up on the beach, and the parents hot on his trail, hunting him down with long knives drawn. He sits down, and for some lengthy minutes only his eyelashes move. 'All right, on three conditions,' he finally announces with terse gestures. 'One, you listen to me, two, you do exactly what I say, and three, you don't do anything else.'

He sits there, admiring his beautiful beach. It breathes softly, to the rhythm of the waves and of the wind that stirs the date palms. The children copy him. They sit and watch. Abid'allah waits, standing up with his arms folded over his narrow chest. Raucous seagulls glide at the foot of the mountains opposite, alighting on the water in a straight white line. Saudi Arabia shimmers on the other side. Other Bedouins, other tribes that own whole herds of camels *and* Mercedes. Darwish's mind wanders, thinking of the people for whom Mecca is the nearest good town to go shopping. Lost in thought, he only moves a toe when a small crab tickles it. Next to him, Juma the clown occupies himself telling two friends yesterday's gossip in sign language.

At last their coach stands up, and the three boys follow, frowning with concentration. Squatting on the coral reef, up to their armpits in the water, they splash out with clumsy strokes, swallowing mouthfuls of sea, but staying disciplined, even Abid'allah.

This lesson from their amateur — and now extra-careful — swimming teacher is to be followed by another the next day, then every day till Friday.

* * *

The familiar north wind keeps blowing, making their hair ripple like seaweed, and stroking the back of their necks. Darwish and his pupils venture a little further out. Abid'allah pokes his head underwater like an ostrich in sand, and everybody laughs, though unknown to him, because he can't see them. Suddenly he ducks even further down. Wondering why, they all stick their necks out and open their eyes underwater: Abid'allah is trying to catch a pufferfish!

They've never seen such an animal before: the masked puffer triples its volume by swallowing water to make itself look more impressive, but really it's timid, and it tries feebly to slip past Abid'allah, who is so fascinated by this soft and scaleless body that he almost chokes. Darwish explains that he has seen such pufferfish before, and even some larger, quite different ones: speckled, blue with black eyes, and some with spines, like the porcupines found in the desert. Muhammad, Juma and Abid'allah are astonished. Every so often they duck their heads back down again, maybe to make sure that this undersea world is still there, with its corals, its seaweeds and its fishes, to check that it hasn't sunk or faded away.

Darwish returns to the beach, his shoulders pulled back like a man with a good job done. He looks at the children, delighted with their new playground, pushing and shoving, skipping about in the undertow. They are looking for the orange crabs and sea urchins hiding beneath their feet in the nooks and crannies of the many-coloured lagoon, and Abid'allah is roaring with laughter.

Abid'allah begins to absorb the marvellous reality, the harmony and pleasure of the Red Sea. With cheerful Juma and solemn Muhammad at his side, he is growing up, filled with this gradually evolving new life. By the age of seven, they are already line-fishing by themselves, standing and sculling as a unit, out for adventure. Fully aware of the precious, exceptional times they are living through, just the way grown-ups do, they make no effort to attend their morning classes. The sea is taking care of teaching them their adult work and life. Like their parents, none of the three will ever learn to read and write; even if the early Eighties start to provide the Bedouins with an organized educational system, the teachers are not trained to teach the deaf, which makes school unbearable. They enjoy themselves signing, playing and scuffling with the other children, but lessons are hopeless.

Yet Muhammad, for one, would have loved to learn. He has always been inquiring and clever, but no teacher has ever bothered to help him. Their difference may be readily accepted inside their own community, but elsewhere it is a handicap, and they learned that lesson young. So the three stick together. Each has his own distinctive character: Muhammad the rigorous, rational one, Juma always fooling, always seeming happy, over nothing. As for Abid'allah, he is the odd one out. Hyperactive but solitary, he listens to no one, not even himself, and speaks only to his immediate family, Juma and Muhammad. He plays on the beach alone, goes fishing alone, and is not yet eight years old when he takes to the open sea to swim and dive, away from prying eyes.

His mother Jamia has stopped worrying about him. Nowadays he is too close to the sea to be in danger. Beside, she has never told him about the *dotora*'s prediction. Jamia's is the only authority he accepts, but while she would like him to fit a bit more closely into the tribe, and try to be more like the rest, Abid'allah will not obey. Every year when school resumes, after a few humiliating days of trying hard to sit there in class without understanding a word that's spoken, he sets off alone to the water's edge. He seems to be hypnotized by the turquoise sea, his everyday resort.

Half child, half fish, Abid'allah has turned into a loner, viewed by most members of the clan as their little savage.

Olin's story

Like three lionesses protecting their cub, the Sinai, the arid Wadi Araba and the Arabian Desert stand benign watch over the Sea of Reeds. The rivers that pump sand into other seas are nothing but shallow dried-up wadis here. Because there is no drainage of sediments and rain-borne minerals, and no river waste, the Red Sea's eco-system is unique, and its water exceptionally clear. Light penetration is high, and transformed by photosynthesis it brings the energy of life to the profusion of seaweeds that live with the corals on the fringes of the sea's coastal reefs, and feed the thousand and twenty species of fishes listed to date.

The ecology of the Red Sea's very numerous inhabitants is nothing like an ocean's. Only a perfect symbiosis allows them to survive despite their fragility. Each creature is useful to another. Certain corals house and protect small crabs whose job is to nip at intruders. Others keep worms that can burn predators with a kind of acid that stops the blood from clotting. If you go diving you will easily see the most routine example of symbiosis: the mutual support of the golden yellow clown-fish, with its two streaks of white, and the sea anemone, a creature like a dark pink flower. If it feels threatened, the fish nestles among the anemone's cream-coloured tentacles like a tired child between clean sheets: coated in slime, it is not affected by their paralysing sting, unlike its many predators. Pairs of clown-fish live in the heart of this soft-bodied animal, lay their eggs around its base, and drive away the butterfly fish that can gnaw off its supple arms.

Further from the reef, the open sea displays another equally striking and more uniform reality. Gigantic shoals of blue fusilier fish with their brilliant sky-blue bodies form mobile landscapes with wild contours sprinkled with yellow. Squadrons of jacks, hundreds strong, throw random sparks across their path. Their vibrant silvery fins ripple with light.

★   ★   ★

It was in the furthest depths of the Red Sea that Olin was born, in one of those moments of intensity when the divine becomes visible, and life exerts its power. The dolphins and

64

their cousins, the bigger Cetacea, are an aquatic mammal order. Along with the Sirenians — the manatees and dugongs — they are the only mammals that make love and give birth in the deep. Tail-fin first, the little pale blue dolphin, weighing seventy-two pounds and already a metre long, slid gently out of her mother's belly, with a few drops of blood, like an olive out of a vacuum pack.

Next to her mother, who kept her distance from the pod, swims another dolphin who acted as her nurse. She helped with the delivery, and more importantly with guarding the newborn dolphin calf. Dolphin calves are a favourite with predators. Until they are two years old they are kept under permanent watch by the mother and the other females who take turns to serve as nursemaids.

Olin swam from the moment she left her mother's belly — though without much confidence. Her nursemaid supported her on the surface with her nose beneath Olin's belly, for the first breath of air. Then Olin went straight into her coordinated breathing training, breathing in time with the adults on the surface. Her skin as a newborn was all creased, streaked with white by her long stay inside her mother's belly, her fins — still soft — turned down and folded on themselves.

The mother did not seem strained by the

delivery: she would have watched the little follower in her wake, while the nursemaid proudly guarded their flanks. Twenty hours after her birth, Olin breathed easily and was already a good swimmer. For the first time, she used her nose to probe for the nipples hidden in two slits under her mother's belly, taken hold of the nipple, and, making her tongue a funnel, suckled on the very rich milk for several seconds. She fed like this, as if drinking a tube of concentrated milk, every half-hour at the start, then less and less frequently, until by the age of two or so, she can hunt for herself. Even when she has grown up, if she happened to fancy some more milk, her mother would have been glad to provide it.

The vast majority of dolphins live remote from human beings, their ships and their coasts, so it is almost impossible to study them. Before the Sixties, and the craze for cetacean research and acrobatics, we knew only what Aristotle had told us nearly two and a half thousand years ago. Thanks to him, it appeared to be established that the dolphin has an intelligence possibly equal to our own, but in any case so different that we seemed unlikely to grasp it. The mystery remains to this day.

I don't truly understand dolphins, and

surely never will, but this is Olin's likely early story. In the light of what is known today by cetologists and by those who fight for their survival about the life of Olin and of wild dolphins in general, I have tried to reconstruct her progress until the adult age when I met her. Olin can't tell me about her past, but I can imagine it . . .

★   ★   ★

Olin is ten days old when her mother formally introduces her to her father and to the family group. From then on, she is a classic social animal. Her survival, food and safety are provided by the whole community: her father and mother, two young males, seven other females and a second dolphin calf, one year old. They belong to one of the big schools in the south of the Red Sea, which contains about two hundred dolphins of their species.

Olin's parents come from the Indian Ocean. She is a Tursiops dolphin — from the Latin 'porpoise face' — also called ambassador dolphins, because they are the species most likely to approach human beings. Like all the members of the pod, she has her own name in dolphin language — a combination of clicks and whistles — which she quickly learns to recognize when her mother or her nursemaid calls her.

Olin has no nest or hiding place. She is defenceless, so during her early years the whole pod keeps a watchful eye on her. When hunting, the little dolphin has to be especially strictly disciplined: sharks like to go for dolphin calves, which they see as easy, appetizing prey, but this is to ignore the ferocity of cetaceans when their young are attacked. Sharks are powerless against them, because the faster dolphins can kill them by combining to ram them in the stomach with their beaks. No sea creature can really trouble them, not even the so-called man-eating white shark. The adults form a permanent mobile shield around Olin and the other calf, carefree roamers whose mother recalls them by whistling their names when they wander too far, and smacks them with her nose when they get up to mischief.

The deeps are scenic pathways, and the group glides along them without apparent effort, but sometimes Olin gets tired. She cries by letting out a continuous whistle to alert the others, like a human baby, and her mother comes racing to help.

Olin loves to swim above her, between the blowhole and the dorsal fin, where she is sucked along by the pressure wave she makes.

As a rule she prefers to stay close to her mother — it feels so good, with constant caresses and attention.

The pod travels all through the south of the Red Sea, and around Ras el Mandeb, between the Yemen and Ethiopia, where the landscape, islands and reefs teem with the striking beauty of East Africa. What a wonderful childhood!

Olin's mother has her memorize the pod's voyages, the dangerous channels and prolific hunting grounds. When the little one follows the pod into a dark fault with enticing contours, her mother makes her practise echolocation, using her sonar, a kind of sound radar that enables her to size up any object or living creature at a kilometre's range. The walls of the fault are just wide enough to let an adult through, then they open out towards the surface. The back light picks out the silhouettes of three big napoleon fish, in their smart parrot-green liveries, greedily prowling near the reef.

As she grows up, Olin sees brown spots appearing on her belly, like freckles. The other calf, her regular playmate, summons her by clicking at her from five hundred metres away, like an audible nod at a hundred thousand hertz. She expresses her delight in playing with him with creaking noises, and he comes charging towards her at top speed, brakes just a few centimetres short, and runs his beak along her body in a long caress. They mimic the courtship displays and fondling of the grown-ups, who encourage them and show them the actions of love, which are meant for reproduction, but are most of all for pleasure: outside their two breeding seasons, dolphins are intensely sexually active.

★   ★   ★

Now is the time for migrations, and the school of Tursiops, in quasi-military formation, covers a hundred kilometres a day on its way to better fishing grounds. Olin is starting to catch her first fish, and already speaks fluent dolphin. Glued to her mother's back like a baby kangaroo in its pouch, the curve of her mouth resembles a broad smile.

Suddenly Olin spots a big cetacean in the distance ahead, then several more, all of the same species. Her mother decodes the echolocation data: it is a small group of Risso's dolphins. They like to keep company with Tursiops, and come swimming to intercept and join them. This is Olin's first sight of a similar species. They travel together. The males decide to exploit their weight of numbers to hunt big fish, and they all set off in tight formation.

Three hundred metres from the school, Olin again hears some large animals that she mistakes for prey till they come closer. These are Sousas, hump-backed dolphins. There are three. From a distance, she knows before she sees them that they have a calf of her own age in tow. They click hello with some funny sounds. When the calf appears on the surface he looks a lot like Olin, in spite of his cream beige skin and small size. But the adults have a ball of fat beneath the dorsal fin, and a coat that shades quite prettily from white to charcoal grey.

The fishing party now resembles a hunt. It is a tremendous feat of organization to marshal so many animals over hundreds of square metres, an extraordinary, spectacular ballet. The Rissos drive the prey towards the centre, where the Sousas and Tursiops take turns to catch them with a single flick of the tail. The adults take their task very seriously, but the youngsters are getting to know one another and starting to play. Olin's mother sees that this time the situation is a bit complicated for their age group, so to take care of the baby-sitting she appoints a young female who is welcomed with a flurry of clicks and whistles of joy and recognition. Of course, the three calves collect their fair share of the spoils, bits of small sharks, mullets and some prawns. Then each school goes its separate way.

★　★　★

The dolphin band resumes its leeward journey, cutting through the water at fifty kilometres an hour. Seeing them coming, a white-spotted red grouper bolts towards a crevice to hide, but the dolphins are sated and ignore their tasty neighbour, which gets off with a good fright. Soft gleams of light cling to the mineral world of a wreck embedded like a spear in the sea floor.

But suddenly a wall is standing and quickly unfurling across their path, where fishermen have released a drift net three kilometres long and thirty metres high. None of the pod members understands what is happening. Olin's parents and three other dolphins are trapped at once in the rot-resistant nylon mesh. They click to their young to stay back. They have to act fast. A Tursiops can only go for twelve or fifteen minutes without breathing, and all five are in danger of drowning. The others take seconds to confer: they surface to fill their lungs with oxygen, then dive towards the prisoners to bite them free of the net, but it can't be done. Their fins and beaks get entangled, and they too find themselves harnessed in this wall of death. Crowded together, with their sonars overloaded, they can no longer understand each other and their environment blurs unreadably. Terror descends. Frequencies clash, the din is unbearable, and panic blocks any possible way out.

'The gods consider the killing of the monarch of the deep as abominable as the murder of man,' wrote the Greek poet Oppian.

★ ★ ★

Olin is paralysed. Stunned by the inconceivable sight of her parents and all her family trapped in unbreakable meshes, unjustly condemned, on the point of certain death, she is terrified. With all her muscles rigid, deaf and blind, now she is lost. She weeps, and continually whistles. In her fright she hears the tumult of desperate clicks and whistles shrilling from each member of her family as every movement tightens the grip of the implacable nylon mesh. Rising above the uproar, her mother's voice orders her to get away at once. Olin has mustered all her energy to skim this last coherent message out of the babble of interference. She understands that she is on her own now, with the other calf who has also escaped the slaughter.

★ ★ ★

Their headlong flight carries them northwards. It is the season of winter rain, and the sea god is restless and dark. They swim fast and deep, carried on the very powerful tide that flows from the Indian Ocean. Already they are approaching the sandy slopes of the reefs on the Sinai coast. There is nothing in their path except for a few busy, good-natured turtles. Sand rays gobble prey unearthed from the sea floor.

Olin and her friend are exhausted. Trembling with fatigue and fear, they swim on, but apathetically. Olin thinks back on her mother's caresses. Her friend comes close and rubs against her. He is gentle. His kindness doesn't erase her sadness, but it enables her to live a bit longer, not to strand herself on some deserted, unknown beach and wait for the end. They swim past Ras Muhammad and come to the Straits of Tiran.

★ ★ ★

Here begins unknown territory for the two young dolphins: the Gulf of Elat. One hundred and eighty kilometres further north lies the bay named twice, after the towns that overlook it: Aqaba, in Jordan, and Elat, in Israel.

Olin remembers her training with the clan. Here she tried to drag a squid out of its hiding place. Her mother helped. It was the first time she had tried it, and it tasted delicious. Some dolphins don't like squid at all. How will she survive without them now?

As they near the gulf, they sense an enormous barrier, an endless wall. Another wall is obviously dangerous. They skirt it, a kilometre out, and locate a way forward on the surface. This is the headland of Ras Nasrani. Above the underwater cliff there is only a single narrow passage between emergent reefs. They glide warily up the sandy slope, but are quickly seized by the waters of the gulf, whose shallow depth and high evaporation creates a suction that pulls in everything coming from the south. Already they are passing west of the Jackson Reef. On their guard, they start to explore the place and prowl around.

Side by side, exhausted, they float in the heart of alcyonarian ranges bathed in light, and shoals of golden butterfly fish. The sun has pierced through the grey clouds, and sits like a crimson ball on the horizon. Olin and her cousin wander. They are empty, but they don't seek food or rest. Like a pair of bowstrings drawn towards the sky, with their special radar on the alert, lost without their family, they are looking for a sign.

They wait for several days, and then the older male begins to fish again. He forces Olin to eat the best fish, and doesn't leave her side for a single second. All his affection is focused on her: she is all he has left in the world.

★   ★   ★

Spring comes with a rush. The sea grows a few degrees warmer. The two dolphins leap out of the water and compete with each other in invention, strength and agility, soaring through the air to spiral over the waves. Life is gradually luring them back. They are regaining their fondness for play, and delight in the silky caresses they exchange. Olin rubs noses with her friend in long kisses, eye to eye. The dolphin presses his torso on hers, but the young female moves away and feigns escape with a double twist. He loops back ahead of her, showing off his litheness and strength, and swims at top speed on the surface with quick, strong beats of his flukes.

For over a week they play like this in the swarming of the reefs' smaller creatures. This morning, with the mist still shrouding the mountains of Sinai and Tiran Island, Olin ventures a little further, and after a few minutes' hesitation her friend comes after her. She sways gracefully under his eyes: the dolphin is a sensual animal. Lured onwards again, he trills with contentment, spins round and glides across the waves to make her laugh, then performs underwater dance figures that happen to end right beside her . . . When he retreats, she in her turn glides closer, practically still, nosing towards him, and skims a long caress under his belly. Then she nibbles at his fins and tail, which brings a few whistles of pleasure.

The dolphin is offering himself, his body curved into an S shape: this is his courtship display. He passes behind her, and turns on his back to place his belly close to hers. Olin dodges. They click and chirp in the dolphin language, and this affection seems to give them a new reason to live.

The encounter

As soon as Abid'allah was big enough to work, he became the ward and general handyman of Lamy, one of the region's prosperous Bedouins. As the custom of Islam requires, those favoured by Allah employ the less favoured, and so share both their wealth and their burden of work.

The owner of some huts on Ma'agena Bay, near Nuweiba, Lamy grew very fond of the boy he called the little terror. His 'hotel' received the first Israeli visitors, hippie types with flowers in their hair. A handful of huts on white sand dunes faced the sea, equipped with nothing but a few canteens of drinking water as their only facilities.

Lamy usually sent Abid'allah out fishing, because ever since childhood he excelled at finding fish when everybody else returned empty-handed. Rising very early every morning, he took both nets and lines in the boat. Generally he wouldn't know which method of fishing he'd use before he reached the open sea and felt the mood of the day. He would scan the horizon, and like a musician reading a score hear his fishing song take shape in his head.

Every afternoon he would deal with all sorts of odd jobs and errands requested by his patron and sponsor. It was Abid'allah who was to be sent out looking for brush-wood and to buy the charcoal or incense for the brazier on which Abid'allah himself would cook special dishes. He also used to serve tea to Lamy and his guests, and build bonfires on the beach to keep the evening conversation going.

In Ma'agena, everyone knew the young deaf man who uttered throaty imitative croaks to express his feelings or attract somebody's attention. Abid'allah didn't speak, he could only blurt out enigmatic noises. Only in sign language could he really express himself, and even if the tourists didn't understand him they quickly took to this impoverished but athletic young man, who also had an unusual gift for free diving.

At times, without warning, Abid'allah used to vanish into the mountains to enjoy their solitude, and to see his mother. Thanks to his earnings from the tourists, he would be able to take to his family a little food or clothing.

★　★　★

In people's minds, the accident was long ago, but for years the gossip at the well remained full of pity. 'Poor boy, it's for sure he'll never marry. It's lucky that he can fish, so he can earn his keep ... ' 'He never speaks to anyone except his two friends, who aren't much better off than he is ... '

Jamia Mekhassen responded to this with silence. She had boundless love for her son, supported his wishes and defended his difference and muteness. In time though, and through her strength of character, she won the respect and admiration of the women, and so of the whole clan. She became listened to, and known to be wise and perceptive. People would come to see her to settle differences between neighbours or cousins who had fallen out. Some husbands even sent their wives to ask in confidence for personal advice.

Little by little, Jamia's reputation rubbed off on Abid'allah. He came to be not so much considered as the strange fish boy, but accepted as the village idiot, sent by Allah to teach men wisdom through the voice of innocence. In societies imbued with Islam, all individuals have their own particular status that brings them respect, and sometimes the less privileged are even credited with magical powers. The blind help the sighted to see beyond the visible, the deaf enable the hearing to listen to the voice of God, and the idiot shows the way to perception. According to the Koran, they are the necessary foils to all the rest; without them people would value their own gifts less.

★ ★ ★

One day when Abid'allah returned from the mountains he ran into his elder brother, Eid, who looked distressed. Abid'allah caught sight of him in the distance windmilling with meaningless gestures. 'It's Mother.' Abid'allah didn't understand. 'What's happening?' Eid sat him down. 'I've been looking for you everywhere this morning. Mother told me that she will soon be dead, run over by a truck on the main road to the harbour . . . '

'Come on, that's silly!' responded Abid'allah, back on his feet and ready to go. 'Why have you got so upset?'

'I arranged with our great-uncle in Bir Zrir to inspect his camels, I wanted to leave tomorrow morning for a few days . . . Now I daren't go!'

Abid'allah sat down again. 'Listen, that's stupid, she only had a dream. Everybody has bad dreams, don't they?' Eid nodded, but without conviction. They parted ways.

A week later, the moonless night was dark and the village in tears.

At eight o'clock that evening, a tanker truck knocked down Jamia Mekhassen on the road. She died at once. Almost soundlessly, perhaps just the rustle of the fabric in her robes and a body falling softly to the ground. The Egyptian driver, tired by his trip from Alexandria, did not see her in the pitch darkness. This was evidently enough to acquit him. Muzeina was appalled.

Caught in a daze, Abid'allah was unable to move. Eid wandered about in the patio, pacing around as if to seek an outlet for his grief. Their father went to ground in one room. He refused to let anybody near, and kept aloof from his children. Among Bedouins, it is not always proper to show grief: endurance is a fundamental value. But although subdued, Muzeina's sorrow was immense. And Jamia's prediction, too quickly fulfilled, brought questions pouring into the minds of Eid and Abid'allah.

Next day, after the midday prayer, in keeping with Muslim tradition, all the families in the Nuweiba el Muzeina clan gathered on the arid plot strewn with grave-stones and big *radjums* to bury Jamia, who lay wrapped in a shroud on the ground. Women wept and howled their common grief. Prayers were said by an Egyptian district mufti. In two files of immaculate jellabas on one side, and black-veiled women on the other, those who had gathered processed towards the grave and sprinkled a little dry earth and a few salt tears on to the whiteness of her last veil.

At the end of the prayer, the south wind rose, as if to bear her away. As soon as the modest ceremony was over, everyone had to take cover. The south wind is rare in these parts. It carries madness, fierce and dry, blowing in squalls that explode on the beaches and devour the coast. When the sky strikes with such force, it afflicts all men and lays them low: they must wait out the end of the storm, huddled in their houses, inside their tents or sheltered behind their squatting camels. For days, it becomes impossible to work or travel: nature must be respected.

When the wind finally subsides, life quietly resumes its course as if nothing had halted it, except for discreet signs like the smiles on the men's faces and the laughter of the women, singing through the patio walls and along the village pathways. But this time the relief was not total, for this wind had swept away a breath of Muzeini air: their beloved Jamia.

After the burial, the entire family stayed inside the tent for a week of mourning. The neighbourhood women did the cooking and made the tea, helping their late friend's husband and children to accept this fundamental fact of our humanity.

With small brief gestures, Eid revealed to his brother the last words his mother had spoken to him: 'Before I set out for the mountains, Mother said goodbye and told me: 'All people who come to you are sent by Allah, don't turn them away. Be kind to everybody.' I keep on thinking about it.' This startled Abid'allah. Why did she have nothing to say to him, her favourite son?

Abid'allah was quick to repeat the words to Muhammad and Juma, who burst out laughing: 'Eid has gone mad! Don't pay him too much attention.' Muhammad added: 'That's a rubbish idea ... if it's someone bad, you have to accept him? Bless your mother's memory, but I don't think she said anything so silly.' But from then on, these words have become central to Eid's life. He draws on it every day, and repeats the rule to any who will listen. As for Abid'allah, deeply affected by Jamia's death, he became a little more unstable than before. They saw him less and less in Muzeina. After catching fish for Lamy, he would skulk out at sea all day long.

He felt more alone than ever, and didn't even want to be with his friends.

★ ★ ★

For his part, his father stayed shut in at home, laid low by sadness to the point of paralysis. But after the week of mourning and a few weeks' seclusion, the older Mekhassen's cousin, the *dotora*, came to see him to discuss Abid'allah. 'You know him, he'll never admit to his pain. He doesn't ask for help, he acts like his father, and shuts himself away. You at home, him at sea. You're both alike. But he is young, and he's wilder and more delicate than you. You've got to speak to him.' Very persuasively, the *dotora* was also intervening on behalf of the other women close to the family. They had all noticed the boy's distress. 'You know how close he was to his mother, but you've never paid him any attention. Today you no longer have a choice. Ask him to come and drink some tea, as a father should.'

The father lowered his eyes. The voice of wisdom had spoken, and he was silent. 'I feel too sad to pay him attention . . . ' he finally proffered by way of response.

'You have no choice,' the *dotora* murmured.

He bowed his head still further. 'All right, tomorrow I'll go and find him on the beach.'

Mekhassen's word. The *dotora* had got what she wanted. She said goodbye, and scurried away from the Mekhassens' patio to another where she could tell the whole story.

★ ★ ★

Surprisingly, the old man knew where to find his youngest son, where the mountains end abruptly, and spill their sand right on to the beach. He strode along the path, his back hunched over his memories.

The sea washed over the pebbles with a faint seething that rose and fell in a sigh of pleasure. When Abid'allah awoke, he had got into the habit of brushing his teeth and going for a swim. The sight of his father there gave him a start. But he smiled. The old man held out his hand and simply kissed him. In sign language, he said: '*Sabahil'kher*, hello! How are you, my son?' 'Fine!' Abid'allah answered, and then corrected himself: 'Well enough, thanks be to Allah.'

'Abid'allah, I'm sad too . . . very sad, but we will go on living so that she can always be proud of us, won't we?'

Abid'allah was caught between laughing and crying; at that point, these were the only ways he had to express how he felt. Sitting side by side, like two friends watching the girls pass by, they stared out to sea, and the open expanses that contain it as if in a mobile, luminous bowl.

Morning and night, Muzeina's landscape changes, and makes each day a different day.

★   ★   ★

For some time, Abid'allah and his brother Eid had been standing in private in the family patio, making broad gestures in deep discussion. It seemed that they didn't want to be overheard, and obviously they had to hide, because sign language has the drawback of being readable from a distance. Yet the neighbours very soon knew their secret — it is impossible to hide anything at all in a Bedouin clan. This must be the reason for the mingling of legends and true stories, and the transformation of one into another, and their circulation in this region. Spreading information like that is the best way to prevent the truth from actually emerging.

The two brothers had decided to build a café, a convivial meeting place, by fixing up the little stone house their mother had left them in the middle of Muzeina beach.

Uncle Ibrahim was furious. 'Eid, it's a silly

idea! Who's going to come to eat and drink in the middle of nowhere? Nobody ever comes to this beach, as you know very well. You'll squander the little money you've got, and Abid'allah what he's never had!'

But Eid and Abid'allah had made their minds up. They bought materials, and every evening after fishing and the siesta they carried on working till nightfall. Their perseverance forced a certain admiration and almost pity out of Uncle Ibrahim, but also from the Suleimans and all the neighbours.

'What's got into them?' they wailed in chorus. Everybody reckoned that their mother's death had unsettled them so badly that they had jumped at the first idea that entered their heads. But their father supported them in their madness: 'They surely have their reasons. My eldest is no fool, and Abid'allah has always had intuition. I want to let them gain their own experience, like we all have.' But he was the only one to do so.

★ ★ ★

After a few weeks' work, the Mekhassens' house stood proudly on its plot six metres from the reef. With its big, old, close-fitting stones, it has a unique charm. So does its unexpected location, and the madness that has placed it there.

The next task was to decorate it. Eid and Abid'allah went to the market on Nuweiba harbour, intending to buy a few Chinese-made cotton carpets from the Egyptian stall-holders. But on viewing the merchandise, Eid remarked that the carpets cost more than the walls of the building had. So they resolved that the floor would be made of fine sand, and cost nothing.

They sawed up old palm trunks which had fallen during the winter storms to mark off a patio in front of the house. They brought in a stove, and some coffee, tea and sugar for the kitchen. Water would be drawn from the spring and stored in canteens.

The time came to wait for the first customers. The two brothers took turns: Eid in the morning, while Abid'allah was out fishing for Lamy, Abid'allah in the afternoon, after the siesta. But their little haven of peace remained empty. Apart from a few inquisitive Bedouins who looked in to see them at work, there was no one — not a single tourist.

'We warned you,' chuckled Uncle Ibrahim, although basically sorry for his two nephews. But with a few well-aimed gestures, Abid'allah sent him packing. 'You're burying us before it's all begun. You'll see, *inshallah*, how this café will turn into a caravanserai for the whole region. They'll all come here to relax, and have something to eat, and to try our beach and our hospitality.' The Mekhassens' neighbours thought they understood Abid'allah's role in all this, confirmed by his reputation as a simpleton: the house was nothing but a clumsy effort to commemorate his mother, at his own expense. But the motivation of his elder brother Eid was less clear to them: older, and supposedly clever, he ought to understand what a mess he had got himself into . . .

★ ★ ★

One May dawn, the men went down to collect their narrow nets, like packets of tangled vermicelli which have to be unravelled and cleaned for every trip. Carelessly thrown over the shoulders of the youngest, Muhammad, Juma and Abid'allah, they magically promise the fate of the catch. Each day, Allah gives a little of his divine creation to the Bedouins to feed them and keep up their faith. Ballotta, swordfish, grouper — ingots and silver coins, treasure wriggling in the bottom of the baskets.

In the boat there was total silence. Not a gesture. All eyes scanned the sea, with the sweeping vision mariners and people of the desert have; looking straight ahead with a selective, analytic eye, the way you do in towns, is no use here. Wide open spaces demand a panoramic gaze that covers at least 180 degrees — that way you will have either the luck or the sheer experience to spot a movement, a change at ten or five o'clock, the shimmer of a shoal of tuna under the surface, or a shark's fin pointing skyward for two seconds. Their small nets were already set between the reefs, and the nylon lines in hand. But that Thursday was not a good day, and nothing stirred between the nets. Fishermen's smiles are gauged by the luck of the moment. 'Allah gives and Allah takes away.' Some days are dreary. In the evening, even if they are empty, the damp nets will weigh as heavy as all the sea. Tomorrow will be better.

At the end of the day, Abid'allah and Muhammad took masks and snorkels out in the boat, to try their luck at diving. Off Point Ras as-Satan, the sun made its regal farewell bow over the rocky peaks, sinking in liquid silence behind those crumbling granite walls. The boys debated in their expressive language, talking about one thing and another, items of gossip. Was Uncle Ibrahim going to marry a very young girl? Exactly how pretty was her face behind the veil? Abid'allah thought she was bound to be ugly, to take such a windbag for a husband . . .

'Something's happening over there,' Muhammad signed, with the palm of his hand at two o'clock. A creature diving. A shark skimming close to the surface — no, there were two of them. 'So close to the breakers is unusual,' Abid'allah remarked. They seemed to be inspecting the boat, from fifty metres away, edging closer in perfect concentric circles. The two young men started to be afraid, and the boat nothing more than a crowded cockleshell. It wasn't funny, and their eyes met with a single idea — to get away. They paddled helter-skelter for the village.

Flames licked the darkness as they sat round the brazier and described their escape to the gathered villagers. The old men nodded their heads knowingly. 'The hammer-head sharks, with a nose like a warthog, they are the dangerous ones, not really the others . . . It depends on how hungry they are, and that depends on Allah.' The sparks of the fire crackled yellow, and darkness spilled into the half-open teapot, where at this late hour the moon also floated.

★   ★   ★

Daybreak called the fishermen back to sea. Abid'allah woke his friend, and their boat nosed into the flat, calm water. Muhammad is a slow riser, but with patience and a Thermos of tea, he gently surfaced. Abid'allah jumped. 'There, to the south, the two fins!' In his fascination, his outstretched arm almost tore loose from his body. He wanted a closer look, and Muhammad lacked the energy to challenge him.

Two things really interest men: to come to grips with death, and to forget it. The two fins, gliding on parallel tracks, seemed to be expecting their guests. Perhaps this made the two of them less reckless in what they were doing. Leaning slightly forward, they stared at that expanse of the sea with their eyes practically popping out of their heads. '*Abu Salam*! They're not sharks! Not sharks!' they repeated, one after the other, as if to reinforce their vision. For one long flabbergasted minute, they even stopped breathing.

Abu Salam, 'Father of Peace', is the Bedouin name for the dolphin.

The dolphin pair moved away, and left two humans lost for words, sitting on their skiff. From that day on, morning and night, Abid'allah never missed a day going to sea to fish. But more than anything, he went to catch sight of the dolphins.

★ ★ ★

The Mekhassens set off by jeep for Ras el
Burqa to cast their nets in the fish-rich waters
where fishing is banned. Since it was Friday,
the holy day of the week for Muslims and the
day of rest for all Egyptian officials, including
naval inspectors, there was no need to
negotiate and bribe.

Abid'allah was leaning out of the back of
the Land Rover, staring into the distance
when suddenly he thought he glimpsed the
two fins out to sea . . . But he couldn't be
sure, since the wind made his eyes water.

The fishing was fantastic, and the elated
family headed back to Nuweiba el Muzeina
with a cargo of fish and squid. On the way
home, the watchful Abid'allah was able to
point out to his cousins the two fins cutting
like sharp blades through the sea, describing
a parallel route to their own, but off shore.
*The dolphins seemed to be following
Abid'allah at a few hundred metres' distance,
even though he was on land.* Flattered and
intrigued, he decided to chance a meeting.

Back in the boat, he was joined by his loyal
friend Muhammad. The spindrift was blowing, and small fresh fish littered the bottom of
the boat. Abid'allah was as excited as ever.
But the dolphins didn't come. Patience and

Allah made no difference.

Back in Muzeina, disappointed, they decided to push on to the refreshment bar, and got drunk on a vodka tasting suspiciously like methylated spirits and completely forbidden by Islam.

★ ★ ★

The next day was nasty — one of those days that make you feel like sleeping till either the Messiah or the Apocalypse appears. Head like a hammerhead shark's, liver like a decomposing octopus, eyes bloodshot and swollen like a pair of pufferfish . . . the sun resembles an anvil, clanging with light, and the ground a floor of quicksand.

To make matters worse, a swarm of startled children came rushing through the streets. 'It's dead! It's dead!' they cried to all who would hear, and they managed to drag half the village with them to the southern end of the beach.

A gleaming smooth body lay there, a vast, sleek, blue-grey mass. An *Abu Salam*, sleeping its final sleep, grounded on the pebbles. 'Allah gives and Allah takes away,' the Bedouins murmured, unable to weep for an animal when life can be so cruel to men, but shaken by the ruin they are seeing.

Abid'allah tried to move the great body, and make it breathe again. The handsome, powerful animal didn't seem to be injured.

Abid'allah wondered how a dolphin could die when no predator had attacked it. 'Where is the other dolphin?' he asked himself. The wise men explained that dolphins and whales had been found before, stranded for no apparent reason on the beaches of Dahab, or on the dunes north of Muzeina. Old Mekhassen shared his experience: 'No one in the sea can kill a dolphin, except for a group of angry dolphins. Even sharks give them a wide berth. Dolphins can kill a shark by ramming it in the belly: a shark isn't fast or clever enough to face them. This one must have died of old age or disease.' Uncle Ibrahim went on: 'It's a common mystery. Sometimes living dolphins strand themselves, one at a time or whole schools of them together. It seems they somehow lose their bearings, through differences in the lunar cycle, or possibly solar flares . . . they can be so set on running aground that no one can prevent them . . . *Allah Ister*, may Allah preserve us.'

Abid'allah was utterly stunned. A bottomless, inordinate sadness gripped him as he gazed seaward, mourning. He thought about the other dolphin. 'Tomorrow,' he signed, with a flicker of a gesture.

★　★　★

The deserted beach, with its endless alternating bands of sand and pebbles, is dotted with sturdy palm trees, each one a welcoming presence that makes life sweeter in its shade. The wooden boat is blue, the colour of the sky. That way, djinns mistake it for sky and do not harm its crew: their evil eyes stray past the Bedouins. It rocks on the waves, with a sporadic creaking from its heavy wooden oars.

Off Point Ras as-Satan, a dark shape skimmed through the waves, like a luminous, little whale. Then Olin came gliding around the boat.

True beauty has no words. It has the smile that comes to those who see it. The shine returned to Abid'allah's eyes.

The two boys swapped disconcerted looks. 'What do we do now?' Muhammad shrugged his shoulders helplessly. 'How do you talk dolphin?' It was Abid'allah's turn to raise his eyebrows. But the dolphin's inspection continued, her eyes and blowhole up above the water.

'She really is looking at us, she's staying

here to talk to us ... ' Abid'allah signed. Muhammad was flummoxed, but tried his luck: he threw a fresh fish as a gift. She took no notice. He tried again: the second fish floated there, equally ignored. 'She's not hungry,' he mimed. 'Perhaps she's sad, because of the dead male, yesterday.' For minutes on end, Abid'allah continued to watch the animal that turned in steady circles round and round them.

With their catch of whiting still wriggling at their feet, they returned to dry land to drink glasses of scalding hot tea. The Red Sea is purple grey at first, at noon, then blues butt in, and sheets of almost vulgar bright neon red, soon to be invaded by shades of evening pink.

In the fashion of traditional fishermen all over the world, many Bedouins can't swim; for them, the depths are a dangerous world where sinister creatures live. The old men therefore advised Abid'allah and Muhammad not to go near the dolphin: 'Nobody does,' Uncle Ibrahim explained. 'Dolphins are kind to men, they are the only ones that protect us from sharks. We Bedouins have never fished for them.' He added with a wry smile: 'But the logic of the sea is not the logic of men: it is the reason of Allah. We men cannot understand it. *Allah Akbar*, Allah is great!'

Muhammad's father nodded. 'Dolphins are unpredictable.' Dusk confirmed him: unpredictably, out there at sea, Olin was patrolling the reef off Nuweiba Muzeina.

★ ★ ★

From then on, every morning Olin shadowed the two childhood friends on their fishing trips, still refusing their gifts of food. They grew used to her silent, graceful presence. Muhammad, the wiser of the two, seemed to stop wondering about the whole thing, but Abid'allah was magnetically attracted, obsessed by the dolphin's daily approach.

Among the Bedouins, there has never been a man who spoke to the creatures of the sea. But Abid'allah is the village idiot after all, and he does everything that others forget to do.

The miracles

Ramadan was coming, a month of fasting by day and feasting by night, and the village was busy preparing. As nightfall drew its first veil over the landscape, the faintest charcoal glaze, Abid'allah waited on the steep rocky beach of Ras as-Satan, kneeling in the oil-black water and skipping small stones across the waves.

The dolphin knew he was there, and looking for her. She breathed loudly, venting puffs of air, and swam closer past the seemingly dormant reef. Her breath sounded like a mellow violin; she was a musician breathing in time with her instrument.

Slowly, Abid'allah came closer. With a tentative gesture, he held out his arm, and she came to greet him, swooping forward to nudge at his hand, retreating and then returning. Again he moved closer. Then she moved away. From the distance her bright eyes looked back at him, before she vanished back into the darker deep. For minutes afterward he remained frozen there, his hand still open and his eyes fixed on the sea.

Abid'allah would never be the same.

He tells how every night for five weeks running they met at nightfall on the beach, touching briefly before Olin swam away. He dwells on these magical moments — the move to a graceful encounter, the same caress, the measure of daily love, like a vital food neglected until now . . .

The children's grapevine soon spread the news all over Muzeina, and marvelling Bedouins came to view the scene in silence, at a distance. Abid'allah's nightly meeting with his dolphin quickly became a legend, the old taking it back to relate when they returned to their mountains. Abid'allah would play with the dolphin, stroking her back and dorsal fin with his palm and fingernails. She would rub against him and then be lost in the blue once again.

★　★　★

One morning Abid'allah dived off his boat to swim with the dolphin, but she moved away. Without hesitation he followed her into the depths, among the undulating corals and their paintbox of colours. The mammal swam slowly, and allowed Abid'allah, an exceptional diver, to follow her for hours. The young man was deeply moved and excited by the proximity of the huge, powerful, peaceful animal, but at the same time disturbed by how very thin she seemed. Surely she must be ill, he thought, for he could even see her ribs. He resolved to bring her a share of his catch.

After the afternoon siesta he threw her some small fish to nibble. It was as though now, having dived together, she could accept this new game. Since dolphins don't chew, much to her protector's surprise she wolfed the titbits in a single gulp. But in time it became clear that the fish weren't the main attraction for Olin: it was the ensuing hug she preferred!

Abid'allah grew more cheerful. He stepped lightly, waved to his neighbours, and had a laugh for everybody. After so many years of gloom, at last his family and the whole village saw their child inquisitive again, and glad to be alive. And playing with the dolphin seemed to open his heart a little further day by day. Muhammad too felt a natural affection for this mysterious mammal. He was also the first to understand the place she took in his wounded brother's heart. Abid'allah was regaining the carefree state of mind that he thought he had lost for ever when he fell out of the palm tree, fifteen years ago.

Abid'allah started to go out to sea several

times a day to find Olin and dive with her. They would brush against each other, play games, and race like children back to Muzeina beach. For hours they could be spotted out at sea, appearing and disappearing, like notes of music on a score. Treasuring her, it was as though he could no longer exist without their meetings. And gradually, he was developing a new language with her. In his deafness, he had always spoken with his body. So it seemed easy for him to interact with a dolphin; their signals and affection in the water are just another language, all their own, physical, sensual, even if difficult for most to learn from outside. They shared a wordless secret.

But Abid'allah also laughed and shouted a lot with Olin. She seemed to adore the loud sounds that the young mute uttered with no real control. He would burst out laughing in the water when she splashed him with a flip of her tail. He would snort noisily, pretending to be drowning; she would push him upwards with her nose and then shrug him away, as if to say: 'I knew you were faking . . . '

He also tried to make sounds to cajole her. He would open his mouth and pretend to speak to her. Knowing the English word 'dolphin', he even tried to call her that, like the others in the village, by miming with his lips.

Dolphins are famous for their main sense organ and chief source of information: their extraordinary hearing, a tiny orifice behind the eye, ten times better than the best human ears. They get tremendous fun out of acoustic games. Yet strangely this dolphin did not speak, or click, or whistle. Had she realized that Abid'allah couldn't hear, and that in any case he would not understand her dolphin language? But she clearly loved to prompt his shouting and laughter, as if they were sharing something. After several weeks of these frolics, Abid'allah started pronouncing vague guttural sounds, close to O and I, without really meaning to. Then, gradually, the dolphin too replied with shrill calls, stroking him with a sweep of her nose or fin, as if to encourage him. This became a new game between the two.

The young man played along with the fancies of the massive cetacean, whose mood would alternate: from clumsy and sluggish, it could change in a flash to swift and alert. Olin also invited Abid'allah to dive deep with her, then zoom very fast to the surface, to take in air. She understood her human companion's more frequent need for oxygen, and offered ways of playing their games that suited both of them.

He continued to mimic words . . . and little

by little, the world began to open up for him: the hearing wiped out since his childhood was even slowly reviving! He didn't really dare to believe it, but the babble of the waves seeped through, and then Olin's calls — her shrill squeaks, her creaking like the purr of a cat, and possibly even some ultrasounds beyond the normal range of human ears.

Afraid of disappointment, he would remind himself that he was deaf, but then when he not only saw the animal's mouth open but heard her cry, he knew he couldn't be making it up. As days passed by and the games went on, the impression of sound grew stronger and stronger — and with it, some heavy questions.

★   ★   ★

That same evening a disconcerted, terrified Abid'allah came running to his father, who was placidly minding the café on the beach. The men come to sit among themselves, breathing the sea air in silence. They enquire of a visitor about his health and his family, and only then ask where he comes from, and what news he brings of the world. They chinwag, smoke the water pipe, and drink tea.

Abid'allah roared in like a cyclone. His father sat him down and signed to ask what had got him into such a state — his child was in tears. He signed back: 'Abu, I can hear!' He pointed to his left ear: 'In there, I'm hearing a little bit.' They all exchanged glances.

Old Mekhassen stared back in disbelief. 'Are you sure? What happened?'

Abid'allah looked out to sea. In rapid sign language, he explained: 'While I was playing with the dolphin, I suddenly realized that I was hearing the sound of the sea, and that sometimes her calls hurt my ear.'

It was as though the silence confined so long in Abid'allah's head had escaped and invaded the gathering. Only the birds kept up their serenades in the date palms.

Uncle Ibrahim surreptitiously tossed a pebble behind his nephew, on his left side. Abid'allah turned round. He had heard it! The surgeon's promise of so many years before, that he would regain a small amount of hearing, had been fulfilled. The silence was transformed into tears barely restrained in the old men's eyes. '*Allah Akbar! Allah Akbar!* Allah is great!' they cried out.

Uncle Ibrahim, the older Mekhassen and the men of the village took Abid'allah to the little mosque in Muzeina, to pray and thank Allah for the hearing so miraculously regained. At the next hour of prayer, the muezzin summoned the faithful as usual, then made several procla-mations of the news: 'Young Mekhassen has one ear back! Allah be praised!'

In the evening, by the light of a big brazier where a sacrificed sheep was roasting, Abid'allah told the audience in sign language all about his experience with the dolphin — his discovery, their approach, their meeting and their antics. The children's eyes were glued to the young fisherman's hands and face; the wise men gently nodded their heads in acceptance, benediction, and little surprise, faced with such a miracle. Among the Bedouins, the old hold many secrets. They can treat numerous illnesses by means of sacrifices and therapeutic trances. They know about apparently insignificant desert plants that can save human lives. Yet from the sea the Muzeini expect nothing but either a scant subsistence or else disaster, and never in Bedouin memory had anybody seen or heard of such an event: a marine animal transform-ing a man in this way. And yet that day's miracle was only the first of an astounding series . . .

★　★　★

Abid'allah continued to spend time every day with the creature he referred to, by rubbing his parallel index fingers together, then pointing at his chest, as 'my friend'. Each morning when he awoke, he would stand on the shore and throw one or two big stones into the water to announce himself. Then he would shuck off his jellaba and plunge into the sea. And each morning she was there: she seemed to be waiting for him, calling out with her little trills. The 'half-deaf', as his dumb companions now dubbed him, then went diving along the reef, and they cruised together side by side.

When he moved away, she'd call him and he'd return; in turn, when she moved away, Abid'allah would raise his head out of the water and attempt to call her by pronouncing the separate vowels of the word 'dolphin' — 'O-I! . . . O-I!' — and she'd arrive!

He learned the way to move air through his throat so as to produce clearer and clearer sounds. All the vowels, and after that certain consonants. Little by little, as weeks went by, he developed a technique of his own, linked to his breathing without his nose under water. He could not fully pronounce the word 'dolphin', because the first letter — a dental — is too difficult, but to call his friend he now uttered 'Olin'. Having regained the hearing he had forgotten, Abid'allah was regaining the speech he had lost. The garbled sounds that he used to produce had turned into words! He was starting to articulate! Was it the daily play training that had given him back his voice? Or the power of affection? Or self-confidence regained?

Still wet, he sat in his swimming trunks on the low wall by the sea, bowing his head, overcome by the further change he had just become aware of. He thought he must be dreaming . . . but he wept. He ran to find Fatma who clasped his head between her large working woman's hands and blessed Allah — Allah and this fish He had sent to release the boy from his misfortune. The news spread like wildfire all over the village. No one could believe it, and everyone came running to listen as, almost in a trance, Abid'allah articulated: 'Olin . . . Olin . . . Olin.' Only Juma and Muhammad were unable to benefit from their friend's recovered voice, yet they were still stunned and gladdened by the miracle, which they still only half believed. Quite by chance, they and Abid'allah had happened to meet 'this big fish' in the infinite sea . . . but was it by chance?

★ ★ ★

The next three days are days of *khafla*, Bedouin celebration. They slaughtered two of

109

the biggest sheep, and drank all the forbidden alcohol kept hidden at the back of the shop. Everyone was beaming; the Muzeini's joy and gratitude were unconfined. Tirelessly narrated, the tale of the miracle passed from mouth to mouth, and lost nothing in the telling. Around the bonfire, the women danced on their own side, and the men on theirs, the children flitting from one group to another, dispensing water and tea. Abid'allah danced, drank, and shouted for joy. He kept repeating 'Olin, Olin . . . '

Those watching carefully could catch him darting furtive glances seawards, maybe trying to spy his Olin's dorsal fin out there, to send her a thought or a thank-you . . . All night long, the drums buoyed up his intoxicated trance.

The rescue

Some months later, an amazing female dance greeted the Muzeini on the beach one morning. At daybreak, a foreign woman had arrived on the beach, unobtrusively put on a swimsuit, and gone diving with a mask and snorkel. The moment she entered the water, Olin arrived to inspect the new swimmer. After a minute of scanning by echolocation, the dolphin sped towards her, and the young woman was soon scratching Olin under her fins or belly, and stroking her tail-fin with her nails. Olin wriggled with pleasure.

The woman dried herself in the sun, got dressed in a long shirt with sleeves and a pair of baggy trousers, and introduced herself to an amazed Abid'allah. Her name was Maya Zilber. Little Salem helped to translate sign language and Hebrew when necessary. The men of the clan approached one by one, and soon the whole village, which had believed that Olin would only let herself be stroked by the deaf ones — Abid'allah, Juma and Muhammad — turned out to greet her. She

111

had captured the tribe that was already calling her *El-Arussat Bahr*, the siren, thanks to her instant friendly contact with Olin.

Maya told Abid'allah her story: 'I live just over the border, in Elat, in Israel, and I heard you mentioned by some people passing through. We are a small group of friends, and near the harbour we've created a place where dolphins swim in the open sea. It's called Dolphin Reef.'

'Dolphins like Olin, near here?'

Abid'allah was astonished to learn that fifty kilometres north of his village, no fewer than five dolphins swam in an enclosure that opened to the sea for several hours a day. Maya added: 'The three females are called Domino, Shy and Dana, and the two males Syndi and Dicky. We bought them from a Soviet research centre on the Black Sea, which was closing down. They didn't know what to do with them, with no budget left to feed them . . . ' Abid'allah said nothing. The thought of buying dolphins . . . It was hard to swallow this woman's far-fetched story, yet she seemed to be sincere, and judging by Olin's passionate response it was certain that she did love dolphins . . . He looked at Maya, quite at ease on the shabby beach, sur-rounded by kindly, curious strangers.

Abid'allah passed on what he had found

out to Muhammad and Juma in sign language. They were obviously taken aback, and he translated their silent surprise: 'We have heard of other dolphins in Israel that swam with men, but we didn't know whether it was true. Olin is the only one we knew . . . ' Maya understood that for people who do not listen to international radio and cannot read, news travels only by word of mouth. 'Come to see us in Dolphin Reef,' she suggested. The idea of leaving the Sinai seemed mad and almost impossible to the three friends, but the other young men who had come over to join them jumped for joy: 'That's great, you've got to go. And you can tell us what's happening over the border.' But Bedouins, like other Egyptians, need a passport — ruinously expensive — to leave their territory. Abid'allah would have to give it some thought. He really wanted to follow this vision, and to meet her Russian dolphins. A new dream took shape in his mind.

But right then, what he longed for most was to understand his friend Olin better. He asked Maya about the way dolphins perceive sounds. 'Dolphins have a system of hearing that humans don't have. They hear ten times more and further than humans with perfect hearing.' Salem translated with rapid signs for his friend, who was fascinated by these first explanations. Amused and delighted to share her experience, Maya continued: 'In a way, they can see with their ears. It is sonar, the most highly developed technique in nature. They perceive sound waves as whistles in their skull and jaw, because of the air passing into kinds of small sacs that each create different sounds. The bulge of their forehead is called the melon. It contains an oily liquid and a small amount of air, which enable the dolphin to tune in on the ultrasounds that it produces. The dolphin sends these pulses of sound, and when they bounce back from the objects they meet they give very accurate information about the type of matter, the distance, the size, and the differences between them. That way they can immediately recognize, say a pregnant woman, or a metal plate in a swimmer's leg.'

'A pregnant woman?' Abid'allah and all the listeners were astonished. 'Yes, certainly. It was thanks to the dolphins that Sophie, Maria and Inbal, our women instructors, discovered that they were pregnant in the very early days. They swam very close to their stomachs, very inquisitive, and used their sonar. You could hear the whistling clearly. They were signalling that something basic had changed inside these women that they knew very well. And even when Inbal entered the water pregnant and brought her partner, they scanned her stomach, and afterwards they scanned the father's sex organs too, to verify that he was the man! It's a shame we can't talk to them and ask them exactly what they are perceiving . . . All we know is that during the first weeks of embryonic development, dolphins and humans are absolutely identical. My guess is that it's this essence of common life that they perceive.'

The Bedouins were spellbound. Salem spoke for them all: 'We had no idea that dolphins had all these powers. Do you think Olin has them too?' Maya nodded. 'Sure she does! She knows a lot about each one of you — for instance whether you're angry or glad, she feels it at once.'

*   *   *

Early next morning, Abid'allah sat by Maya's bed, visibly anxious, waiting to question her further when she woke up. She had barely had time to register his presence when he started up. 'Maya, Olin isn't sleeping any more. I watched her all night, and she never stopped swimming.' He spoke with the speed of his urgency, and Maya could hardly make him out. It was so early . . . She mumbled: 'But Abid'allah, a dolphin never sleeps.'

Abid'allah was stunned. 'Never sleeps . . . ?' He thought Maya must be trying to fob him off, so as to go back to sleep. 'Maya, Maya, all animals sleep at least for a little while, at least in winter . . . ' Maya could see that that night's sleep was definitely over. 'Abid'allah, dolphins' brains have two sides, just like ours.' She drew a diagram in the sand. 'Breathing is a conscious decision for a dolphin. That means that if they sleep completely, they stop breathing, they sink and they die. So they sleep with one half of the brain, and then the other. They swim all night long, and if you like they sleep in two instalments.' Seeing her pupil's jaw drop, Maya went on: 'Also, the most developed part of their brain is the one where the feelings, creativity and love are located. Unlike man — well, usually, I don't know about you . . . ' she added, and laughed — Abid'allah had just received his first anatomy lesson, the first in a long series, in fact. He knew that no matter how close his friendship with Olin, he was no cetologist, and in Maya he had found the expertise he lacked, to help Olin if she should ever have a problem. He had confidence in Maya, and by extension in the whole team at Dolphin Reef, which he soon started to call his 'friends and advisers'.

⋆　⋆　⋆

Some weeks later, while Muzeina's quiet, humble life continued under its desiccating sun, Olin was threshing around in the water ten metres from the beach like a panic-stricken puppy caught in a flood, uttering squeals of alarm. On shore, time had stopped. Three Bedouins dressed in immaculate jellabas and traditional keffiyehs, sitting cross-legged in the shade over their game of back-gammon, looked at each other in dismay. Three seconds went by in a daze, then Uncle Ibrahim sprang to his feet like a grasshopper and raced flat-out for Abid'allah's hut, to the south of the beach. Tapping him on the shoulder he signed 'Olin — Danger.'

The young man sprinted towards the reef, spotted the panicking dolphin, tore off his jellaba and dived in to join her.

Olin was clearly afraid. She headed northwards, out-paced him, stopped and waited, then set off decisively again, utterly sure of her direction. Straining his nerves, Abid'allah followed, having no idea what was wrong, knowing only that she needed him somewhere out there, as fast as possible, and that was enough. Finally, just a few metres away, he saw the rogue net. Drifting loose,

117

sprawling over kilometres, they will accidentally trap everything that lives.

A dolphin, a young male, was caught in its nylon meshes, whistling and struggling hard. He must have been chasing a fish, and got tangled in this deadly trap. With snout and tail immobilized, he was still breathing, but painfully. Abid'allah tried to tear the netting apart with his bare hands, but without success. It would need a sharp knife . . .

He put his hands between the meshes and the animal's blue-grey skin, and rocked, leaning alternately right and then left, trying to release him. Then he pulled at the shuddering mammal's snout. After two or three minutes that passed like centuries, the head was free, but the tail still trapped, holding the dolphin down. One fluke was cut, and oozing a thick white liquid, like the sap of a rose.

Olin could do nothing. She swam around them as they fought, one against dying, the other, with his human hands, desperate to save a trapped friend. Perhaps Olin's nightmare memories of childhood were coming back — the memory of the slaughter, inflicted by mistake, mere indifference, or in wanton extermination of thousands of whales and dolphins. This is the toll taken by the thousands of deep-sea trawlers whose nets drag the ocean deeps, and of the all too numerous nets left illegally drifting at random, unseen, bringing their daily sentences of death to whale species all over the world.

Even though he had never practised free diving as a sport, because of his playing and fishing under water Abid'allah had become an exceptional diver who could stay submerged for record lengths of time. Even so, after three minutes he had to resurface to breathe before diving again. The seconds continued to pass. Abid'allah tugged and heaved. At last it worked. The dolphin was free! With one bound the captive propelled himself skywards like a ground-to-air missile. Oxygen poured into his lungs.

The wounded dolphin then remained on the surface, weak and gasping. Olin was soothed and relieved, but Abid'allah was wiped out, his arms refusing to obey him. Olin swam in between them, lifting the man's shoulder or the dolphin's rostrum with her head, supporting them above the water to help them to breathe without effort. The weakened young dolphin started to move slowly. He made several tight circles round the man, taking his leave, then swam away.

Olin brought Abid'allah home; he clung to her dorsal fin and allowed her to pull him along. When they arrived, she waited by the shore with her eyes above the water, as if to make sure he was safe — or regretting having let him leave the sea. Perhaps she had heard the story of the Little Mermaid, who for love of a prince wanted to replace her beautiful tail with a pair of human legs, and died for her wish . . . She stayed on in the water, but on the near side of the reef, with her body only half submerged and almost on the beach, at a depth of half a metre.

* * *

There is no rational explanation for such a chain of behaviour: a dolphin calling a man to the rescue to save the life of another dolphin, relying on his hands and on his good will. I think that, for a dolphin, to save the life of a mammal has nothing to do with kindness. For them it is an act of natural solidarity, even if the recipient happens to belong to a different species. I have consulted many books looking for similar recorded examples, but without success. History certainly abounds with examples of dolphins helping humans in distress, ever since ancient times, but there is no report of incidents when they have appealed to a man to help them, even though that must happen more often than people believe. Some fishermen kill dolphins to sell them, or in sheer indifference, while others do their best to save the mammals when they are not their target.

It does seem that dolphins retain the 'memory' of such actions. Almost two millennia ago, Plutarch told the story of a man called Korianos, a native of Paros, who sees a whole school of dolphins caught, and persuades the fishermen to let them go. Several years later, his own ship is wrecked on the coast. The whole crew drowns, but one man survives, carried by dolphins to the safety of a cave: it is Korianos, whom the cetaceans have not forgotten. Later, when he dies, in the sight of his astounded family and friends, the dolphins appear to bid him farewell: a few metres out from the shore where his body lies burning, they blow and wait for the last embers to fade before heading for the open sea. Plutarch writes: 'The dolphin has no need of any man, and yet he is the friend of all men, and has often brought them valuable aid.'

In 1997, a dramatic event was the talk of Abid'allah's own region. Not far from Elat, a slightly tipsy English tourist fell into the water and was injured by a yacht's propeller. He was bleeding heavily, which seems to have attracted several sharks. They had him surrounded, and he had given himself up for dead, when a school of Tursiops dolphins, Olin's species, formed a defensive circle, drove off the sharks, and saved his life. They brought the injured man to the first boat they spotted in the bay. I don't know what became of the man. Did he carry on drinking? Or did he become a cetologist . . . ?

All these episodes remain exceptional and mysterious to humans. Most likely we will never know the motivation of these cetaceans that sometimes link their lives to our own. All the same, we can see that in most of these situations it is a case of one individual facing another. I don't think that dolphins necessarily love human beings, rather that particular dolphins choose a particular human to play with, care for or help. There's always a personal story involved, a close relationship, a friendship.

Since Abid'allah discovered Olin, several scientists have tried to unravel the logic of their amazing experience. Neither Bedouin nor Western observers understand the phenomenon. There is no academic explanation, and apparently no precedent in either that region or elsewhere. In Muzeina, the elders have absorbed the genuine friendship between Abid'allah and Olin, and expanded on it. The Bedouins cultivate their tradition of chants in verse, and verbal contests in polished Arabic: true stories quickly become splendid legends that travel down the centuries and over the mountains on donkeys' and dromedaries' backs. They change, evolve and propagate from village to village, and convey the teachings and strict ethics of Bedouin culture.

Certain inhabitants of Muzeina are convinced that Olin is none other than a messenger of Allah: like a prophetess, they must listen to her, and try to understand her teachings and her prophecies. No one in the village has ever been introduced to the great myths of Greece, and yet this is exactly what they describe, in a pagan version: to the Greeks, dolphins, allies of the god Apollo, were the earthly, privileged messengers of Olympus.

The wise Ibrahim, the uncle that Abid'allah calls the egghead, thinks that Olin is not really an earthly creature but an angel inhabiting the body of a dolphin. 'Oh, there've always been dolphins in the Red Sea, for sixty million years. Long before the Bedouins, long before humans. As well as the Tursiops, Olin's kind, there are any number of Risso's dolphins, false killer whales, Sousa's dolphins, also called hump-backs, and dugongs or sirenians,' Uncle Ibrahim explains. Then he raises his eyebrows. 'But Olin is a miracle!'

Eid, Abid'allah's elder brother, sees in Olin a very particular angel. He immediately recognized in her the reincarnation of their mother, Jamia, who died just a year before Olin's appearance in the life of Muzeina. He says that he saw Olin some months earlier, on Muzeina reef, accompanied by three young dolphins. Now he has confirmed with his father that Jamia had lost three daughters at birth. He thinks that she met them again in paradise, and brought them with her to visit the village. Eid finds this extremely moving; this miracle opens new perspectives on his mortal life. According to him, his mother has returned to help her favourite son, the one of whom it is said that he was the least spoiled by life: Abid'allah.

More wonderful lessons

Muzeina, spring 1995

The women brought their empty buckets back to the well, deep in conversation. As they hauled on the rope, their voices mingled with the creaking of the big wooden pulley. Each of them was seeking to marry off a youngest daughter or an eldest son.

And of course they were talking about Abid'allah. Now, pity has made room for mystery and a certain admiration. *El-bedu*, the people of the desert, respect Abid'allah for the fantastic gift he has received. Allah has bestowed this special prize, he is the man who talks to dolphins.

Muhammad's mother was reminiscing. In the old days, when she was small, the families were nomads, they had nothing but their tents. And then the sea drew the men away from Muzeina, like a curse. She repeated to herself: 'A curse struck the men of the tribe of Muzeina. Little by little they became fishermen. At first they fished so as to dry enough fish for the winter. Then they started to abandon the mountains, abandon their desert. And then, as the years went by, my father and his whole generation built houses, the way the Israelis did, and the Egyptians . . . Oh, of course we kept our tents and herds, the goats and camels, and we often went off to the mountains.'

Today, the women claim that the men wanted permanent houses because of vanity, but in the husbands' view, it was the wives who wanted more comfort.

That is how the little palm grove to the south of Nuweiba became Nuweiba el Muzeina: 'Our beach of date palms became our fathers' village . . . the fishermen's.'

According to her, the other tribes summoned and publicly rebuked them: a sedentary Bedouin is no longer worthy of the name, and his tribe can no longer be part of the confederation. Soon, the traditional assembly of the *kabilat*, the ten Bedouin tribes of the Sinai, voted unanimously for 'Eba'ad! Banishment!'

Since then, Muzeini can no longer marry members of the other Bedouin tribes, or take part in the assembly of the confederation. Condemned to keep to themselves, and to marry among cousins, congenital deficiencies have appeared: this is no doubt the explanation of the high rate of deafness among the Muzeini.

'Ya! My aunt! No one remembers when or why we, the Muzeini, were banished! It was ages ago!' protested Khadija, a first cousin of Muhammad. She explained her point of view: 'The other tribes of the Sinai have been less and less nomadic for some time . . . anyway, at least since the Israelis came in 1967. Remember, Aunt, even the Dahabs and the Tarabines started to work with them in the greenhouses, the fields, or other places . . . and then the Egyptians brought the tourists in. I was at school myself. There were other tribes with us, and already they were only moving their herds in the winter months.' She paused to think. 'Perhaps we were banished for being the first ones to build . . . but it was so long ago, nowadays all Bedouins go to and fro between their tents and their houses . . . like us.'

All states have attempted to settle their Bedouin populations — the Syrians, the Israelis and the Egyptians. In Saudi Arabia, too, it is a rare group that still moves its herds to winter pastures. Of the great camel-driving tribes of bygone days, only shadows remain: the Huweitat, the ancestral masters of raids and plunder from the wadis of Wadi Sirhan, the 'godfathers' of the desert who attacked or protected caravans and oases according to the *khawa* paid. According to Lawrence of Arabia they were the finest fighting force in all of western Arabia. And the Ruwalas of the Hawran desert in Syria, Iraq and northern Jordan still live as nomads in the old way, but are fewer and fewer in number. Yet among the dunes and mountains of the region's deserts, often the traveller catches sight of encampments of black tents, woven from goats' wool. Along the roads, near Jerusalem, the oasis of El Jafr, or around Ma'an in Jordan, the Bedouins bring their families and their camels. Elsewhere, they probably have a house by a well, or with running water and electricity provided free by the government. But in summertime they prefer to move and pitch their tents where it suits them best.

Abid'allah represents the first key new element among the Muzeini since their banishment. They who thought themselves cursed for ever interpret this incredible event as a sign from heaven. Abid'allah may be the messenger who will release their *kabila*, their tribe, from its sentence. His speech regained may also be the speech of his whole tribe.

Like the Muzeini themselves, the legend of Olin and Abid'allah is fixed but its soul is completely nomadic: it spreads through the mountains of the Sinai and the coast of Sharm el Sheikh to Elat across the border, up to Tel Aviv, and gradually out to the world.

* * *

On a jaunt to Dahab, the town ten kilometres
south of Muzeina, where the tourists are
numerous and often pretty, Abid'allah came
across some other people of the desert who
recognized him from the tales that had gone
before him — the young man from Muzeina,
in love with a dolphin. They hailed him,
determined to see with their own eyes the
wonder they had heard about.

They suggested they drive back with him
by Jeep to the beach at Nuweiba el Muzeina,
now commonly known as Dolphin Beach.
Abid'allah needed no persuasion, only too
proud to have signs of such warm recognition
from these members of another tribe. Among
the first to run into the legend on its path
across the far desert, they were impatient to
witness this famous friendship.

Olin's fin swept through the waves coming
off the beach like a sunbeam through dark
clouds. Her energy flew across the sea, and
her presence spread over the reef and on to
the pebbles. The children paddling in the
water were calling to her in the distance,
curious and a little bit afraid. But she stayed
far out to sea, in the glow of the sunset.

But when Abid'allah appeared under the
palm trees on shore, the purposeful fin

headed straight for the beach, as if by magic. She was waiting for him. He rushed to meet her, forgetting the others behind him, his white teeth gleaming in a grin stretching from ear to ear.

Olin leapt a metre above the surface. The sight resembled some sort of implosion, or a firework turned to water, as their two beings met and embraced like two magnets pulled together. The Bedouin visitors heard the deaf man's roars of laughter and saw the joyful splashing. Outblazing even the heat of the sun, the warmth of their friendship reached them all. In their turn, these nomads from another tribe were absorbing this lesson in love.

★ ★ ★

From town to village, to Nabek or to Sharm el Sheikh, the witnesses have passed on the story of the Muzeina wonder, and passing strangers who happen to talk with those villagers hear about the dolphin that goes swimming every day with a young man. Curious to see for themselves, some take the coastal road in search of this isolated place — with no hotel or tourists, where no signpost points and no tarred road leads.

By questioning passers-by, at last they find

their way to a bare shore overlooked by a small stone building, the Mekhassen café. Welcomed like lords, the pioneer visitors decide to stay for a while by this flat, secluded beach.

After coffee, tea, *tahina* — sesame seed oil paste — and *musakhan*, pancakes of well-baked Bedouin bread covered in pieces of chicken and onions fried in olive oil, spiced with paprika and sumac, the visitors face seaward and look for the dolphin. 'Remember, it isn't a male, it's a female!' Abid'allah explains with his characteristic passion and enthusiasm. He pronounces words slowly and with obvious difficulty. But the syllables emerge one by one, deep and guttural. In the calm of Muzeina, listening with respect and attention, it is easy to understand him.

The whole Mekhassen family — the father, Uncle Ibrahim and Eid — were amused and pleased by what was happening. Olin was drawing their first customers, bound to come their way when they looked for her. The café once doomed to failure, marooned on a beach where no one ever came, was acting more and more as a meeting point: the dolphin caravanserai. The tourists enjoyed sleeping in the open, and took all their meals there, cooked by Jamila, Ibrahim's skilled young wife, except when Abid'allah also lent a hand, because his main concern was to make his first 'foreign' visitors' stay unforgettable.

In a few days he introduced them to some of the magical, mysterious sights of the Sinai's north-east coast. First the Blue Hall, an undersea cleft so deep that it seems bottomless. Even as you swim on the surface, above the chimney that you have to enter one by one, vertigo may surprise you. You feel ambushed by the blue night below, though as yet you see only its upper edge, a small coral reef teeming with sergeant-major fish in gold robes striped with black. You follow Abid'allah as he glides into the crevice, and then plunge headlong into the depths, towards the rock basin just under thirty-five metres below. Sunlight and barber-fish accompany you, and the back-lit scene is beautiful. You hang totally weightless under a breathtaking rockscape.

After some time to rest, Abid'allah takes the visitors on to Shark Bay, unquestionably the most impressive diving site in the world. There you walk in light sandals over fire corals whose slightest touch will burn the skin for several painful hours. When you reach the wall of the reef, you scuba-dive above the pink, blue, green and yellow seaweed of this rugged coral barrier, eight hundred metres deep, whose countless recesses make lairs for roving predators. Sharks often visit these waters, and nobody ventures too far. Sometimes an exceptionally violent current sweeps up shoals of immense barracuda, tuna or snapper that maraud in the dark blue limpid eddies of the Red Sea depths, until the coming of their enemies, the silky or hammerhead sharks.

But Abid'allah has discovered with amazement that for many visitors all the wonders of the Sinai count for nothing compared with spending a little while in Olin's company. Rapture for them is the sight of her dorsal fin cutting through the tranquil sea.

Every morning, Abid'allah arrives at their usual meeting place and calls out: 'OLIN! OLIN!' The sounds are unsteady, but his guttural voice is loud and resonant, almost fearsome. After a minute or two, the dolphin appears behind the coral barrier . . . Then he takes his ecstatic guests into the water; they swim close to Olin, and witness the extraordinary undersea dance of the two lovers. Soon their faces are wreathed in huge smiles of durable delight.

★　★　★

One morning, Eid and Ibrahim Mekhassen were returning from the Um Zarib valley carrying supplies of dates and olive oil in wicker baskets on the thwart of their boat. But more than five hundred metres out from Muzeina, the little motor spluttered, stalled and gave out. Both men were exasperated: neither of them swam well enough to reach the land.

They looked at each other. Would they just have to sit and wait to be rescued? There was no point in shouting, they were too far out. Maybe someone would spot them from the beach. After a few minutes, they felt a presence in the water. It was Olin, who seemed to be inspecting the boat. Ibrahim picked up the mooring rope and threw it into the water, trying to make her realize that she should go and fetch Abid'allah.

How do you talk to a dolphin?, they were forced to ask themselves. Much as he loves riddles, Ibrahim was puzzled. Here he was, facing his nephew's best friend, and he didn't know how to explain the situation! To Eid's immense surprise, he started shouting very loud and clearly, leaning over the water, nose to nose with their graceful spectator: 'Abid'allah! Abid'allah!' You never know, he said, she would have heard his nephew speak his own name while he played with her, when he was feeling very joyful, glad to be with her and to have the power of speech. But the

Abid'allah is an exceptional diver. Since his accident he was always a loner, spending his days at sea by himself...until Olin entered his life.

One of the oases of the Sinai where the Bedouin of Abid'allah's Muzeini tribe spend time during their migrations, and where over the centuries they have established citrus groves, and cultivated vegetables and dates.

Above left: When they leave the mountains of Sinai to return to the shores of the Red Sea, the families leave their tents and other household effects they don't need for their next return, several months later.

Above right: Ahmed, Abid'allah's cousin, tells their story in sign language. One in every seven Muzeini children is born deaf, so sign language is a mother tongue.

The first evidence of the friendship between Olin and Abid'allah: a solitary fin apparently following the young man, waiting for him every night in the bay. Abid'allah was intrigued by the sight, for dolphins usually live in groups out at sea. One day, he went out to meet her...

Above left: One of Olin's favourite positions since she and Abid'allah came to know each other: vertical and motionless in front of him, she's just asking to be hugged before threading her way down to the deeps, Abid'allah by her side.

Above right: Squid is Olin's great treat. Abid'allah catches a few for her every day when he goes fishing; she finds it difficult to dislodge them from under the rocks herself.

It was on the occasion of one of their gatherings around a
great fire that the story of the 'miracle' began to pass among
the Muzeini. The legend of the little boy who began to
speak again took form, and soon spread across the desert...

Above left: Abid'allah with Asher, an Israeli to whom he owes
a lot. It was Asher, Abid'allah's father's employer, who came
to his aid when he fell from the palm tree. His own family
had no means with which to help him.

Above right: Maya, the cetologist from Dolphin Reef at Elat,
a great friend of Abid'allah and the one he calls his 'advisor'.
She came to help when Olin was in poor health. Dolphin
Reef has welcomed a group of ambassador dolphins.

In December 1996, Olin disappeared. Abid'allah was beside himself. But when she returned, she brought with her a tiny double of herself, who had come into the world out in the open sea. Abid'allah named him Jimmy.

Above left: On the beach at Muzeina it's hard to ignore the tourists. Thousands of people now come from all over the world to marvel at the dolphin 'miracle'.

Above right: Abid'allah takes his guests swimming with Olin in small groups. She plays along in good grace providing the visitors aren't too pushy. All it takes is a swipe of the flukes to send them reeling.

Left: Abid'allah with some of the mail he now receives from all over the globe.

This little stone hut on the beach (left) was all Abid'allah and his brothers owned, left to them by their mother. Once Olin's fame was established, Abid'allah set to building a hotel to receive visitors on the site (main photograph). The impoverished and sidelined fisherman is now one of the tribe's most important people.

Abid'allah and Olin, the two heroes of this amazing story. For a wild dolphin to choose to stay permanently so close to a man, without any coercion, is unique – and a testament to the power of friendship.

name made no impression on Olin: instead, she circled the little boat once again, and then she found the mooring rope, slipped her beak inside it, and started to tow the boat slowly. Eid and Ibrahim could only sit and gape as she ferried them five hundred metres to the reef, and solid ground.

Abid'allah was not there to watch the exhilarated tribe applaud the procession. And Ibrahim is still coming to terms with what happened! Very little is known about the motivations of dolphins. Abid'allah thinks so too, and gives a shrug — 'Sometimes I don't understand her' — and it doesn't bother him at all, because Olin can express her wishes to him.

★　★　★

It seems to me that the deep identity of dolphins and their magical relationship with men will stay locked up for ever, like a vital riddle. Yet we know that we can compare them to a baby who is in synaesthetic tune with the surrounding world, and is thought to perceive its whole environment as one. Sounds, colours, shapes and textures combine into a single packet of multi-dimensional information. The dolphins' sonar, that extraordinary echolocation device, makes this work of perception a more unusual process, however. Dolphins naturally perform dozens of correlations in space and time. They live within a conception of the world that has nothing to do with the one we know.

Yet for fifty years numerous researchers have come a long way with their experiments. The different approaches tried in the effort to understand cetaceans, dolphins, killer whales and whales are fascinating, because all those who have encountered dolphins at close range have seen their fortune change. I have tried to read up on people whose stories might shed light on the future in store for Abid'allah, and I have found some disturbing personal histories.

The greatest defenders of the cetaceans are often former experts on captivity, and on capturing them at sea for dolphinariums. John Lilly, an expert on human — dolphin interactions, Jim Nollman, the crazy musician who communicates with them through the tunes he plays on his electric guitar, and other more classical zoologists, like Paul Spong and Louis Herman, do not always agree about the results, or the methods, of research, but together they offer a basis for deeper understanding. They estimate that dolphins use only ten per cent of their large brain to collect the varied information they require, while the other ninety per cent processes, plays and reacts with that information. They might as well become the mascot of all those poets who, ever since Baudelaire, have pursued the supreme goal of achieving the total sum of their sensations! In Lilly's view, it is as if a dolphin is in a permanent state of advanced transcendental meditation. He interprets their communication, by sonar among other means, as sendings of erotic nerve impulses.

Jacques Mayol, the first man to have reached a depth of a hundred metres under water without an aqualung and whose story inspired the film *Le Grand Bleu (The Big Blue)*, tells in his book *Homo Delfinus* how his emotional history with dolphins made an early, decisive impact on his life. A single event in the Red Sea made its mark on his future. When he was seven years old, he and his family were on board a liner crossing the southern Red Sea when, standing on deck, he saw dolphins for the first time. The child thought at first that they were sharks. This often happens: a kind of ancestral fear affects human beings, something carried in the collective memory; the sight of a fin in the sea immediately means a shark . . .

After getting over this initial shock, Mayol and his brother were baffled by the apparent puffs of steam emitted by the animals' blowholes, only a few metres from the ship. He writes: 'What struck me most was the bright eye, full of intelligence, the eternal smile, and the near-human sound of their breathing ... I had sensed that we had something in common, that they were rather like brothers in the oceans ...'

Mayol has much in common with Abid'allah, who in this sense can certainly take the name of *Homo Delfinus*, Dolphin Man: an innate sense of the sea enhanced by passion, enforced by strenuous work transformed into play, exuberant energy, a very distinct individual personality, and an almost magical contact with all animals. An image strikes my mind: what if Abid'allah Mekhassen were to meet Jacques Mayol ...? Maybe they would only have to swim together to know one another. Or maybe they would have little to share, being basically too alike to have something different to exchange.

Mayol also describes the decisive event that made dolphins a model for him: one of his disturbing experiences with Clown, the captive star of the Miami dolphinarium where he used to be employed as an assistant. One of his chores was to clean the interior windows of the big dolphin pool, Clown's world, her living quarters and her prison. He used to go under water wearing a diving suit and carefully polish the plate glass windows that enabled spectators to watch the animals' daily life and wheeling flight. He was very attached to this dolphin, and they played together every day.

After some months, he noticed an incredible coincidence that it took him several weeks to believe. When he was in a good mood, Clown would come and nibble at his clothes and have fun with him. When he was bored, or sad, or thinking about his personal problems, she would pass behind him, pat his back with her flipper, and leave him to it. And when Mayol was in a hurry, and aiming to finish off his work as fast as possible, she would never come near him. It seemed that Clown could always read his inner state of mind. 'Man can't always explain everything,' Jacques Mayol comments. He believes that dolphins are all equipped with a kind of telepathy among themselves, but also with human beings.

The only Dolphin Reef instructor who thinks like Mayol in this regard seems to be Inbal. Over the years, she confides, she has been through too many similar and disconcerting experiences to deny what she now sees as obvious. She grew up in Tel Aviv, where the sea was her playground. As a child, she earned pocket money by selling the fish she caught. 'My dream as a little girl was to play with Flipper ... but I thought you had to speak English, the way they do on TV, to be with dolphins. Today, the dolphins are my best friends, and we don't need a word to communicate! I believe that I understand their moods and their wishes. Certainly, when I'm not concentrating they keep their distance. On the other hand, when I very much want to be with them, we converse through some games we've discovered together. It works by body language and expressions.'

Inbal readily speaks about telepathy with cetaceans. She told me an amazing story, though she also advised me to try the experience for myself — which I did, without success. She adores seahorses, those tiny floating dinosaurs, and one day when she was sitting on a wooden platform at Dolphin Reef, stroking the snouts of Syndi, Shendi and Domino, she fell to thinking about them. She was training all three dolphins, but she had always been specially close to Domino, who slipped away, but returned a few minutes later with a small live seahorse flopping on her tongue. 'Then she opened her mouth to present it to me!' Inbal smiles. She is used to hearing herself described as a dreamer in

Elat, but she is quite certain about the kind of life she is living with her dolphin friends.

Mayol's experiences with Clown, and Inbal's with Domino, have an essential point in common with the case of Abid'allah Mekhassen and Olin: their relationships are based on mutual trust and key moments of true intimacy. No one knows why, but Abid'allah was incapable of facing up to intimacy with another human being, whereas with Olin he could develop a genuine bond. Yet there is one major difference: Olin is utterly free, and her human contacts totally voluntary. Abid'allah and Olin are both at home, in Muzeina and in the Red Sea, free to come and go, each of them choosing whether or not to be together. For this, they have the whole of Bedouin temporality, all the time they need. An hour can become a day, and then a month. And above all they are both their own masters. Their lives are independent. Abid'allah and Olin live their relationship on an equal footing.

Though we know that in the history of humanity there are ambassador dolphins who approach men and women, this remains an absolutely exceptional occurrence: very few dolphins choose to spend some fraction of their lives in contact with one or several humans. Those who are captured are real hostages, prisoners for life of human fancy. They do not survive very long in their closed pools, and tend to die young.

Olin and Abid'allah found each other; two solitaries met and grew together. Many sought a rational explanation for this bond. They saw Olin as a dolphin rejected by her species, some sort of outcast who had found in Abid'allah the only creature who could take an interest in her, and vice versa. But the future would disprove these hasty judgements.

Thwarting destiny

Abid'allah and Fatma were sitting almost face to face on the colourful carpets spread across the beaten earth of his forecourt. She was reading the curves and patterns of the coffee grounds left on the inside of his glass. Fatma spoke indirectly, almost whispering. She had discerned the childhood prophecy made by his mother, and murmured: 'Abid'allah, you must beware of the sea.' She saw Olin cutting through the waves. 'My son . . . she is going to leave.' She looked up at Abid'allah, ready to repeat what she had just said, but he had understood, and turned pale. He sprang to his feet, and made straight for the sea.

When he found his friend, he wrapped his arms around her and clasped her tight. He swam with Olin throughout the afternoon, and even the pooling dark of nightfall did not drive him from the water. If he could turn into a merman, or any marine mammal, he would not have hesitated for a moment. It is amazing to see him in perfect symbiosis with the sea, an environment that many consider

143

as hostile. For Abid'allah, its deadly, vindictive surroundings mean comfort, shelter and pleasure.

Human fish, or seal, or dolphin? Abid'allah goes his own distinctive way.

★   ★   ★

'She can't leave . . . I would be desperate without her,' Abid'allah declared to Juma and Muhammad, sitting cross-legged on the sand, his back to the northerly breeze. 'In all my life, that's all I ask from Allah: that He should leave me Olin . . . ' Tears streamed down his tired young face. He was so unhappy, a feeling he had forgotten. He thought he had banished sensations of menace, foreboding and unease for good. But Fatma's prediction had plunged him into depression. His friendship with Olin was no longer an exceptional piece of luck, or even a gift from God; it was a revelation that had opened up his life. Without her, he thought he would die.

Juma tried to reassure him. 'She won't leave. Why would she suddenly leave? She's fine with us. I swam with her only today, and she loves us.' Abid'allah flared back: 'Fatma doesn't make mistakes!'

Muhammad the moderate, the thoughtful one, knows his friend well. He anticipates his follies, and was already considering how to convince him not to give in to fear. Abid'allah needed to stretch his legs, so he stood and took a turn round the beach. When he got back he found his two friends in the same position. They looked up with worried expressions.

'We're going to make her a big net,' declared Abid'allah.

'You surely don't intend to shut her in a cage?' Muhammad protested.

Abid'allah pointed southwards. 'A net that reaches from your father's house at the end of the beach, Muhammad, to just north of Nuweiba, by Madane's place.' He seemed relieved by this solution. 'A very big net,' he insisted. 'That way, she will feel comfortable and we will be certain of keeping her.' He pounded his chest decisively. He had thought it all through, and a smile of childish pride lit up his eyes.

With drooping heads, Muhammad and Juma stared blankly at the sand, helpless to deal with their friend ... What light of wisdom could illuminate somebody who had never listened to anyone but his mother, who was dead? Muhammad felt caught either way. Oppose Abid'allah's will? Unthinkable. Help him to fix the net? His heart forbade it. How could they confine such a creature, who came to bring gladness to the village of her own free will? But Muhammad suddenly realized how attached he had become to this animal, too. She had changed his own life as well. Of course, he himself will never hear, but he now sees further into his surroundings, and into his own feelings.

The night is short, and on the beds where the three friends lie a few metres apart on the beach, their brightly patterned woollen blankets perform a restless, insomniac dance. They toss and turn but cannot sleep, and peace of mind seems far away. The prophecy lurks in the shadows and turns them hostile. Even before the early morning mist, typically excited, with the last few pounds of his pay in his pocket, Abid'allah set off to buy hemp rope in long skeins.

A few hours later, the advisers from Dolphin Reef showed up — Maya, Sophie and Oren, all with determined smiles. Muhammad must have called them on the phone, helped by one of his brothers who can hear.

Abid'allah was very glad to see his friends, his 'great advisers', again. 'What's new?' asked Maya innocently. He launched straight into his plan: 'I'm going to shut Olin inside a big net, like the dolphins at your place!' Eyebrows shot up, and eyes swapped wordless questions. Maya, respected for her excellent relationship with Olin, had her say first. 'Abid'allah, till now you've been the smartest. You've managed better than we have. Stay with it! Don't be fooled by some people who'd like to influence you.' Abid'allah, up-front as usual, replied, and quite proudly: 'The net is my own idea!'

'Your asset is your relationship with Olin. If you confine her, you'll change everything. She'll be unhappy, and you won't be able to be friends any more . . . '

Abid'allah stood up thoughtfully and went for a glass of tea. The debate lasted all day long, villagers joining in, then going off to work and letting others take their place. Everybody in the village had listened to bits of the argument, everyone had had his say. The elders saw the situation as going beyond Abid'allah. They wanted to reach a communal decision. 'This has become village business,' said Sheikh Ramadan. 'The wise men's council will meet tomorrow.'

Maya summed up for Abid'allah the difference made by the forty kilometres of coast that divide Dolphin Reef from Nuweiba Muzeina made. 'You have what we dream about building, we're building what you dream about having. Our business is your dream, your friendship with Olin is still ours!'

147

By the evening, Abid'allah had lined up with his advisers' point of view, and opposed the net. He informed the elders: 'I've thought it over, and Maya is right. The net is bad for Olin, so it's bad for us all. You don't shut in the hand of Allah!'

But the next day dawned with a cool breeze, a clear sky, and a host of questions for the village. Muhammad sat waiting for the wise men's verdict, even though deep inside he longed to run straight to the beach to help his friend: Abid'allah was standing in his boat, ready to make a bolt for the sea with Olin in his wake beneath the hull. His mind was made up: he would do all he could to keep her free. If the council came to the wrong decision, then both of them would leave.

Opinions were very divided. 'One day she'll be gone, and we will be back where we started again,' Sheikh Ramadan asserted with authority. 'We can't lose this creature, she's too valuable. Bedouins are travelling a long way to admire her, and it makes them respect us. We are the Muzeini, the tribe cursed for generations. No other Bedouin can marry a daughter of ours. This gift could put an end to our banishment.' His eyes shone as he heard himself speak, and the others nodded their heads gently under their traditional red and white chequered keffiyehs. Madane picked up the theme: 'So we could string a fishing net all the way from the sea wall facing Abid'allah's cabin to the Atwas' land. There'd be plenty of room, and our boats would berth a little further north.' Madane was born in mid-migration and he always thinks practically. But Uncle Ibrahim hesitated: 'Madane, it's possible, it's feasible, but the question is not how we do it. The question is, have we the right to do such a thing?'

'How can we imprison what Allah gave in his Greatness?' Old Mekhassen suddenly exploded. 'That dolphin may be the reincarnation of Jamia my wife, bless her memory. You want to shut her up in nets, when we don't even hobble our camels! We leave them free, like brothers. You don't keep Allah's creatures tied!'

A shiver chilled the bubbles in the two hookahs. The soft sound of air bubbling through water always calms the mind, and the scented drift of their aroma brings wisdom. The water tobacco-pipe passed from mouth to mouth in a healing calm.

All the major decisions are taken in this circle. When the argument is deadlocked, the last word goes to the sheikh.

Silence spread, like a healing balm. The

elders were lost in thought. Then Sheikh Ramadan spoke again, in solemn tones. 'For fear of insulting Allah unintentionally, we will leave the dolphin free to come and go. May Allah be with us.'

'*Amin! Amin!*' the tribal elders chorused. The gladness in their eyes spilled out across the sand to Muhammad, who sprang to his feet with a face as open as the sky. He signalled wildly to his friend offshore — 'It's all right, it's all right!' — and plunged in to join him. 'No more net! No net!' They hugged one another, united in gladness and relief, then they set off to swim and play with Olin, who seemed to share their good mood without knowing what she had just escaped from. Abid'allah couldn't stop repeating: 'I'd never have let them do it, never, never!', and Muhammad kept quiet, as usual, and simply smiled.

★   ★   ★

It is the enlightened choice: freedom for the dolphin, risk for the Muzeini, the risk of losing what they thought for a while they could control. The old Bedouins have understood that by shutting dolphins in and attempting to control them, by trying to keep them so close they had only to reach out to touch them, they would destroy the essence of their captives: their wild state, and the truth it preserves. Of course, all the men and women in the world who keep them in confinement are fond of the dolphins in their care. They give them all their love, but it remains a jailer's love. There is a Hebrew saying that out of every evil comes a good, no matter how slight . . . It is true that thanks to dolphinariums and the thousand dolphin prisoners of today, Western public opinion now feels concerned about the future of cetaceans in the world.

Muzeina beach, winter 1995

Abid'allah threw a stone at the reef to warn Olin of his coming. But Olin hadn't kept their morning rendezvous. Abid'allah, Muhammad and Juma were all set to go, the usual small fish thrown into the bottom of the boat . . . but Olin had disappeared.

Abid'allah flew into a rage. Muhammad felt guilty and hung his head. After all, he too was responsible for Olin's freedom. As for Juma, for once his usual role of clown or scapegoat seemed too dangerous. He took his young cousin to Nuweiba harbour and treated him to a *fatir*. There's nothing to be done, he thought, she'll be back . . . On some days his stubborn optimism could cheer people up; on others, it could only redouble their pain. Yet this time he too was afraid, afraid that these events would separate the inseparables, Abid'allah, Muhammad and Juma, the three deaf friends who lived on the shore. Fatma's prediction was looming like a stormcloud over the Sinai.

★   ★   ★

Day two without Olin. The three sit side by side on the beach, attended only by the glimmer of a candle in the pitch-black night, their presence signalled by Muhammad's breathing, Abid'allah's smouldering eyes, and Juma's fingers fidgeting in the sand. Despair is setting in.

★   ★   ★

On day three, the colour of the morning is like Olin. The blue-grey sky has dulled the turquoise sea. Abid'allah has resurrected his mask as the poor ill-tempered idiot of the village, with a glint of defiance in his eyes. The others are sad, just sad. The whole village — the women in their patios, the children playing on the beach and between

152

the tents, the old at prayer or sleeping, people passing through — everyone is waiting.

★ ★ ★

Day four. Wednesday. They wait on in silence. Bedouins can leave silence untouched. They respect it just as much as speech. Hours spent wordless with a stranger are sometimes worth the closest attentions. You don't hurry a man or woman of the desert, or force them to yield to any law but their own: they would rather die. Like dolphins, so it seems.

Here, respect is gauged entirely in details and in truths. What you give is rightfully yours in return. What you receive is yours for ever. And the sharing is your life.

Olin did not stay in Muzeina by accident. Perhaps she chose the Bedouins even before she met Abid'allah, or perhaps the values she came across here inclined her to stay close to these people of the desert — even if they still can't swim, and throw bottles and plastic bags to the wind.

★ ★ ★

The fifth day is the thumb that closes the hand of fortune. 'Allah gives and Allah takes away' is on all lips, and slowly He helps everyone back to life. Abid'allah still goes out fishing, and brings back nothing but squid, which are hung to dry on the clothes-line in Olin's absence. He no longer sleeps or eats. His tears taste like dust. He scans the horizon, and now and then throws pebbles in the sea . . . to attract the one he calls his wife. He listens to none of the anxious villagers, and his pain rubs off on his friends. All three wander around looking dismal and hurt.

★   ★   ★

The sixth day, Friday, the holy day, ends the week. The muezzin calls to prayer. His chant summons and entrances the faithful: 'Allah is great, *Allah hou Rahman*, Allah is merciful.' Abid'allah rises and goes to prayer for the first time, causing stares of surprise. The Islam of the Bedouin people is moderate. They pray and keep their distance from the dogmas and muftis based in towns.

★   ★   ★

Both in the Bible and in the Koran, on the seventh day God rested. His servant, Abid'allah, has collapsed with fatigue and grief under the palm grove on the beach.

But it is eleven o'clock in the morning, and

154

the sun at its zenith throws warm shifting patterns over the slant of his cheek. Suddenly Muhammad is stooping over him like an eagle on its prey. Abid'allah turns over with a jerk, and as Muhammad keeps on pestering, he hauls himself up on one arm, ready to deliver an angry slap with the other. Then through his half-shut eyes he sees the radiant look on his deaf friend's face. Now he gets it.

The wind dries his tears as he dashes to the sea. She has returned.

★　★　★

The mosque hummed with joy. The murmur of prayers formed a great stairway that could have lifted Abid'allah all the way to paradise, if he had not been too afraid that to climb it would take him away from the sea and his wife. His tears were full of sunshine. He hugged neighbours in the street, both men and women — well, the women in his family. He gave all his small change to the children, who revelled in the snap celebration.

Abid'allah went round telling everybody: 'Olin went away to punish me for wanting to shut her in.' He walked tall and his smile had returned: 'I'll never do it again. She stays free, and that's good. If she wants to go, then fine, let her go. If she wants to return, then welcome. She is free.' He was happy, and his self-confidence was back. Yet Olin's disappearance had brought a change in him: he felt that he bore a responsibility towards the dolphin, and decided to take five or ten kilos of live squid and fish from his catch every morning to give it to her.

Abid'allah had matured. 'I love her, I love her, and she loves me too!' he shouted to all he met who didn't yet know him. He did not mask his pride: 'Olin is my wife. If I marry, she'll go away for good.' His father hung back when he could, to explain to whoever would listen that of course, his son was joking.

Muhammad too had changed. He now dared to say how close he felt to Olin, even though he did not launch into rapturous statements of love, like his friend. And if Abid'allah was gradually becoming the figurehead, the spokesman for Olin and the village, Muhammad was keeping things going, on the days when his hyperactive friend dropped out of sight.

New arrivals

Some strange new faces have started to appear in Muzeina. Women and men with big packs on their backs, dressed in jeans, with scarves tied round their fair hair. Often these fearless travellers have peeling noses from exposure to the scorching sun in their quest to take in their surroundings, and to make their future memories stick. The smile they all share — of people who are tired, and glad to be tired — makes them look alike. They know they are going to find what they are looking for, because they are looking for anything interesting they can find. These passing strangers incur the traditional hospitality of the Bedouins, who soon perceive the cause of their sudden interest. For tourists, Muzeina itself has always been the least attractive spot in the Sinai, and the Bedouins know it. No beach of white sand, as in Ma'agena Bay, and no truly exceptional undersea sites . . . To the north and to the south the surroundings are perfect: so why stop here? But now they stroll in twos and threes in the village lanes, and ask in English, Hebrew or stumbling Arabic where they can find the beach 'with the dolphin man'. Many do not even know their hero's name.

Full of their experiences, Abid'allah's first guests have described their trip back home, and so stirred up a tide of interest. Little by little, groups of friends of Olin and Abid'allah have formed in Europe, Australia, and Israel. And they make the pilgrimage in order to come and marvel for themselves.

Children or elders bring the tourists to the small restaurant built by Abid'allah and his brother Eid. On the pebble beach, by the weatherbeaten old blue boat, the rough stone cabin has an air of pride. After all the jeering it came in for, and the anxiety, its presence gives a focus to the unique friendship whose story has travelled round the world.

Muhammad greets them, as he greeted me the first time, with his kindly, generous silence, his glasses of tea, and his neatly placed carpets, bordered by fallen date palm trunks. A few metres away, from the far side of the reef, Olin is a docile apparition. Already she haunts the imagination of the people who wait to see, approach and touch her. But often they barely catch a glimpse. 'And you touch her? You play with her?' the visitors invariably ask.

After serving tea, Abid'allah and Muhammad take their curious guests on board their blue boat. Proudly, and partly in show, the young men dive with Olin, watched by spectators mesmerized by the reality of this dreamlike vision. The rumour is true! They really are friends! Fascinated to be so close to a wild dolphin, and impressed by the power of the current that passes between them, they will never forget the scene.

★ ★ ★

Since Olin's arrival in Muzeina, a young scientist called Oz Goffman has been landing there regularly, taking photographs, jotting down details in a notebook — always the same one, apparently — and leaving again. Naturally he started to be recognized on the beach, and the locals gradually realized who he was. He runs the Israel Marine Mammals Research and Assistance Centre (IMMRAC) in Haifa, less than five hundred kilometres across the Israeli border.

As the first weeks went by, he answered all the questions that Abid'allah and Muhammad had been asking themselves about Olin. It is from him that they learned that their friend is about twenty years old, as shown by the small white markings round her snout and her big worn teeth. The two boys have never studied zoology, and never had the chance to observe other cetaceans in captivity or even at liberty. They cannot read or write, in any language. All they know is Olin, her own language, and their sign language. So they have informed him about Olin, and Oz too has become a friend and adviser. And for anyone who knows Oz Goffman, that is an achievement, because this *doctour* is above all a scientist.

The exchanges went well, and Oz is a very regular visitor. He has become Olin's vet, or at any rate her insurance. If she has any medical problem, they call either him or the Dolphin Reef advisers, and they try to take care of it.

By summer 1996, Abid'allah was feeding Olin every day, so Oz offered to teach him how to train the dolphin to repeat the natural leaps and acrobatic figures that she would perform to catch fish herself.

One morning the three friends found themselves kneeling in the little blue boat, glad to be together and nervous about the outcome. To begin with, Olin stole the first demonstration fish by snatching it gracefully while the *doctour* wasn't looking. The tension rose slightly, because it should be up to the trainer to control the situation . . . The role of the animal is to follow the instructions step by step so as to leave the man the illusion that he is really running the operations.

Abid'allah held out a second fish in his hand, only just above the surface of the glossy sea. Olin observed the game and glided past the bait, her sonar on, trying to fathom the cause of all the fuss. Seeing nothing suspicious, on her third pass she snaffled the fish. Then it was Muhammad's turn, guided by Oz; patiently, he kept holding his hand higher, offering a tastier fish at every stage.

It took three whole days for Olin to deign to hoist her two hundred agile kilos out of the water. The fact was that she had no *need* for this food that her friends were providing. All she wanted was their love and attention. It is because she enjoys being stroked and encouraged that she consented to tackle these new drills.

First at fifty centimetres, then at two metres high, she leaped out of the water, and brought a burst of applause from the villagers and visitors watching on the beach. Most of her body is muscle. Its power makes her soaring aerial spins look easy, and her curving figures force gasps of admiration. But the wonder runs highest when Abid'allah is leading the game. Then Olin summons all her verve and energy to satisfy her friend, and give a great performance.

Now Oz is no longer sure whether he has

done right to point the Bedouins in this direction. His amusing little exercise could quickly turn into a top-flight tourist draw, but that might jeopardize their relationship with Olin. Abid'allah was very enthusiastic about the training, but the daily workload, the dolphin's moods and his own quick temper sometimes get on top of him. Muhammad decided to involve himself no longer, and the training has rapidly become his brother's preserve. 'He's afraid of having Olin taken away from him, he's jealous, and it drives him crazy!' Muhammad told Oz. But finally the dolphin spectacular satisfied everyone, especially the tourists.

Muzeina beach, autumn 1996

Abid'allah had returned with a wriggling catch. 'Forty kilos!' he boasted, holding up the hoop net. He was exaggerating a bit, but everyone now knows his measurement system: they take away a zero and multiply by two. Everything was ready — the fish, the boat, the weather set fair, Abid'allah the trainer motivated by some Dutch girls who turned up yesterday, Muhammad at the stove. All were looking forward to the afternoon dolphin show and acrobatics, after the siesta. When the tourists were seated on the beach, Abid'allah stood up in his boat and held out a fish — a baletta. Olin reared up and tried to catch it, but she only rose halfway from the water, and a second and third attempt made it obvious that while she was gliding beneath his outstretched arm, she wasn't leaping. She wouldn't make the slightest jump above the surface. It was as if she had swallowed some lead. Her anxious trainers concluded that she wasn't well, in spite of her usual fondling, and the fact that under water she seemed completely normal. Muhammad claimed that she was eating too much, and it was true that she had gained some weight — everyone had noticed. 'Abid'allah,' rapped Muhammad, 'you're overfeeding her, you've got to stop these extra fishing trips.'

Abid'allah got angry, and went out fishing again anyway, but this time for market. Muhammad bustled around his guests, who were disappointed but not disconsolate, sprawled on the carpets. Their noses were already less red in the northerly wind.

★   ★   ★

'I don't think Olin is fat, I think she has her stomach full of life. She's expecting a calf.'

163

Doctour Oz's words were a bombshell. Then last winter's disappearance was the moment of her baby's conception? If so, she would give birth in December, because a dolphin's gestation period is twelve long months . . . In a flash, the time it takes the children to whizz round the village at top speed, like cartoon mice, the Bedouins gathered on the beach were in uproar. 'Olin can't have made a baby on her own!' cried Uncle Ibrahim, his jellaba tails flapping in the wind, while Ramadan and the other children laughed under his nose. 'Other dolphins must come here at night,' Madane supposed. Oz could not give her an ultrasound scan, and hoped that he wasn't mistaken. But in any case, despite the surprise and joy, no one really believed it. 'Allah is great, but truly, this would be even greater,' cried the older Mekhassen in confusion.

When Abid'allah returned from his fishing trip, the rumour hit him and he set off shouting with delight. 'I'm going to be a dad! I'm going to be a dad!' *He* had no doubts, and went flying along, arms outstretched in the eye of his personal cyclone, like some self-igniting fire-work. 'Life is beautiful!'

★　★　★

Weeks and months passed by, with no more aerial leaps or training sessions for Olin. Visitors were told that they were witnessing a new miracle, and Olin was pampered more than ever by her friends. The visitors were disappointed, because the dolphin story had grown with the telling, and people were expecting a show like the ones put on in the big specialist centres in the USA and Europe, where all kinds of captive cetaceans are put through their paces. 'We are a village,' the sheikh explained, 'and the animal is at liberty, no one makes her do anything. She's pregnant, and we're lucky to be able to go near her in that condition.'

The sheikh was feeling tetchy, however. He was getting more and more caught up in the whole dolphin affair, no doubt carried away by the wave of easy compliments on foreign tongues. The truth was that he would readily have pushed her to perform, but first he would have had to go through Abid'allah. For his part, Abid'allah was lavishing attention on his 'wife', whose slightly swollen belly was no longer changing, and was giving no sign of what was about to happen.

* * *

On 28 December, Olin vanished once again.

The weather was stormy. Haunted by bad memories, Abid'allah and Muhammad put to sea to look for her. Broken clouds marbled the sky above their heads, and the icy breath of the rare west wind swept across the land, threatening the sailors with those numbing rains that come with the frozen touch of another, lifeless planet, yet amazingly cause new plant life to burst from the ground. For two days they wandered at sea, passing the surface glints of great shoals of fish — tuna and different kinds of blue fusiliers — but they were not tempted to put even one line out for dinner. The sun would break through and cheer them for a moment before disappearing, maybe for twelve hours at a stretch.

As the second afternoon closed, an uneasy, tearless gloom descended. Suddenly the two friends' eyes were caught. Olin was there, in the trough of a wave, swimming north-west, heading quite slowly for Muzeina. 'Could she be injured?' asked Muhammad from the stern of the boat. Abid'allah didn't answer, he was already in the water. He kicked his bare feet skyward like a fish's tail, diving beneath the surface. The sight that met him below the waves made his heart skip a beat. By Olin's broad right flank swam her small-scale shadow. A dolphin calf, a mammal baby, sixty centimetres of dolphin. A small tail fin, a small blowhole on top of its head for breathing, a cute snout, that classic, built-in smile of all her kind. Olin in miniature, without the freckles. Stunned and transfixed, Abid'allah hardly dared to move.

She approached, her calf hugging her side. She presented her little one to him, as she would have done to the leader of her clan, yet he did not dare to touch her. Still in shock, without a word or a sign, he hauled himself into the boat again, his eyes still glued to Olin, and explained to his friend about the unseen new arrival. The two followed in their wake to the village, the half-light silhouetting the forms of the men standing on the shore, jellabas flapping in the wind, waiting for the wanderers' return. They already seemed to know what had happened. The intuition of the Bedouins travels long distances and draws intricate shapes and pathways — it is an intrinsic part of the mystery of that proud nomadic people.

This was the first time in the world that a wild female dolphin had given birth to a calf so close to a human environment. She introduced her young to Muzeina as if to the members of her own clan. That night, yesterday's young victim of misfortune was once again the hero. The bonfire set his hands moving, and a hundred times over, in a poetic dance of sign language interrupted by shouted phrases, Abid'allah told the story of his meeting with the son of his 'wife'. Eyes shone with gladness, and the big fish sent by Allah the Merciful was blessed and blessed, over and over again. The Bedouins wished health and long life to the little one and its mother, who were recruited that evening into their clan, their tent, and of course into their ancestral stories. The children stayed up late, and slept by the fire — except for little Ramadan, who was greedy for every word spoken by his cousin Abid'allah.

The following day was a holiday, and the next days holidays too.

Among the women, hot tears of joy were shed. Only Fatma was silent.

★ ★ ★

At sea and at the well, the weeks went pleasantly. Abid'allah named Olin's little one Jimmy, after one of his own cousins, born in America. God bless him, the dolphin calf grew a little bigger every day. He was growing fast, and Abid'allah's reputation grew with him.

Soon after Jimmy's birth and alerted by the

grapevine in this region of the Levant, where everyone knows everyone else's business, the cameras arrived, and people asking strings of questions. Day by day, press and TV news teams from all over the world converged in quick succession. They each handed out stickers to the children with the logo of their respective programme, like climbers planting their national flag on a mountain peak scaled for the first time. The little ones stuck them on their skin like transfers and forgot about them, a lot more interested in the masses of high-tech equipment.

Festooned with cameras and mikes, the reporters prowled the beach looking for stories. The Bedouins tend always to see them as actors rehearsing the same scene: a taxi arrives from the frontier or from Cairo. The cameraman emerges, followed by the sound engineer and by the journalist paying the fare. Sometimes an Egyptian Arabic interpreter comes with them. Dazed by the journey and the heat, they look for a place where they can get something cold to drink, and pick up information.

They settle on the beach, in the shade of the palm leaves at the only café, built by the Mekhassens, and start their inquiries. 'Where are the big names here?' they want to know, after a refreshing glass of some imported beer, and invariably the waiter answers: 'I'll tell you the whole story. I am Abid'allah, Olin's friend.' Wow. 'Him, the waiter, Abid'allah? But this guy can talk,' the strangers murmur in their various languages. Of course, for anyone who knows the story, Abid'allah's progress is terrific, for every week he speaks his Bedouin Arabic a bit more clearly than the week before. And perhaps most surprising of all is that he already speaks a smattering of Hebrew and a few words of English.

Abid'allah was quickly crowned king by the media, the king of Muzeina. His story and its miracles grabbed the TV and radio headlines in neighbouring countries, and photos of Olin and Jimmy were front-page news in the world's newspapers. Not only that, but Olin seems to love being filmed or photographed. I wonder how she perceives the camera, what she hears in it, but in any case she really performs for it. With her snout almost kissing the lens, she brought her offspring to help make a record of his early infancy. He looked like a light green lettuce, an undercooked finger roll, a darling, fragile bud.

'I'm married to Olin, Jimmy is my son. And if I married another woman they would both leave,' Abid'allah repeated over and over again. Even the tape recorders registered the smile of the young man who never tired of telling the story of his life, or at least the side he wants to show.

As the spiral of publicity propelled Abid'allah's fame across the region, the months passed peacefully, visits becoming routine. The journalists covered village and beach in a few strides, stopping only to grab an interview with Uncle Ibrahim or some other villager. Behind the courtyard doors and walls, not far from the village square, the women would watch and listen as the next wave caught their men.

The flatness left by the departure — as sudden as their coming — of these busy media bees gave a feeling of letdown. Abid'allah, Muhammad and all of Muzeina found themselves musing about these strange and uninvited whirlwinds.

Whether they are journalists, cetologists, artists, dolphin-lovers or all sorts of experts, each person who comes to this beach finds a reason to be interested in Abid'allah's small seafaring family. They have renamed him Abdallah, which is more convenient for them, and he has even begun to use the new version himself, but I feel that it is wrong to change his name. I call him what his father, friends and neighbours do: Abid'allah, in Arabic the servant of Allah.

It is thanks to this invasion that I got to hear about the saga of Muzeina. From my very first visit I was captured by the place and its inhabitants, by Abid'allah and Muhammad, and most of all by Olin. The fantastic 'true legend' of Muzeina has possessed me ever since. For my film, to write this book, and then simply because I have friends there, I soon came back, to share, write, and attempt to understand.

This media frenzy that crosses frontiers seems natural: the fantasy aspect of this story fascinates everybody and injures no one. The exoticism of the place and the life of the dolphins simply add an upbeat note to the weather reports.

On the other hand, for the Egyptians who rule the Sinai, the issue is more complex. Quite apart from the tourist promotion that boosts the region's development and the influx of foreign currency, media coverage may help them to gain the hold they long for over these impervious renegade tribes. How are they to get a grip on this desert society, as hard as the region's granite and as soft as its birds' song? Its laws seem changeless, fixed in the collective memory for centuries, and passed on by the words of wise men. The confederation, the great tribes, the clans, families and individuals support each other, argue, and always make peace again. Like a thicket of reeds, they grow up together in a harmony that, though it may look chaotic seen from a day-to-day viewpoint, is also very solid. Only the Muzeini rule the Muzeini. Neither the Israelis nor the Egyptians nor anybody else will impose laws that go against their grain: either they will pretend to absorb them, or they will set off with their camels to some far reach of their rugged mountains. A Bedouin does not kneel to any stranger. He listens, and mostly lets the silence do his talking.

Yet the Egyptian authorities are doing their utmost to control, settle and pigeonhole them, even to conscript them into the army. Represented in the Cairo parliament by the most ambitious among them, they still know practically nothing about what goes on there. Except that sometimes a Bedouin needs a passport to cross the border, and then, after endless red tape, the state demands five hundred Egyptian pounds (about fifty pounds sterling), a prohibitive sum. So the Bedouin is now effectively condemned to stay inside the frontier of a country, even though for him the other side is also part of his migratory grazing grounds.

The authorities were soon trying to exploit the dolphin phenomenon, pulling the rug out from under the locals. On the square in Nuweiba el Muzeina they built a monumental statue, standing on a tall stone plinth, of two stylized dolphins caught in mid-leap, nose to nose, with their tails touching so as to make a heart shape about one and a half metres high. And not very far from there, they also constructed a luxurious mosque, to impress the Bedouins with their devoutness. Islam does appear to be the one point in common between the Bedouin tribes and the Egyptian people.

★ ★ ★

With the wave of international professionals, attractive young foreign women of a curious character have also started to show up in Muzeina, or more precisely at Abid'allah's place. When their Bermudas and bare shoulders emerge from inside a decrepit Egyptian taxi whose driver, clutching a bunch of crumpled notes, seems peeved with himself for letting this vision escape, the children ask in their makeshift English picked up from previous tourists: 'Dolphin? Abdallah? Want to see?' Then the oldest grab the bags of these tall blonde women, and the little band sets off.

After settling in their rudimentary huts, out

come the bright or navy-blue bikinis, and the half-clad bodies that stroll to the beach and are offered to the gods of the sea. Nowhere else in Egypt, even on TV, is there a sight like this to be seen. The mermaids of the West have landed in Muzeina. The Bedouin women feel a mixture of envy and pity for these foreigners who don't even think about their dress and who look desperately trustful under prying eyes. Bedouin women only go bathing in their own company, wearing their thick robes, and they wade in up to their bottoms and no further. Sometimes they sit down to play with their children just far enough out in the water to feel its touch between their covered thighs. Bedouin women don't travel by themselves, and incidentally they don't travel at all beyond their own vast deserts. They are strong, and they rule their men and children at a distance with an intuitive remote control which is more like the dolphins' marvellous sonar than any listed human sense.

I find it hard to understand how this Bedouin society managed to stand so many changes, in so short a time, without something cracking. The women have laid no restrictions on their husbands, and cast no spells. I feared that a wave of hate and trouble would break over the village, but no such thing has happened. The Bedouins, men and women alike, have accepted the Western Martians with their seasoned sense of difference. It seems to me that the pride of their independent culture has enabled them to welcome others with open arms, and a tacit acceptance of the consequences. The old have even allowed the younger generation to take on new responsibilities without infringing on their choices or their rights. This takes my breath away. I think about that ancestral reputation of the nomads, their adaptability and sense of survival, and I believe that I recognize that a little miracle happens every day in Muzeina.

The next generation

Muzeina beach, March 1997

When Jimmy was three months old, Olin started to show him how to fish, giving him scraps of fish to taste, as well as suckling him. He swam above his mother's back to use the pull of her slipstream, and save his energy. They travelled that way a lot, and when he was tired she would support him on the surface with her snout, so that he could breathe as much as he needed to. It is a beautiful sight, a dolphin calf with his body still pliant, sitting like a small roll of carpet on his mother's protective rostrum, surrounded by the little blasts of air from his surface breathing.

Olin no doubt also taught her son who the humans were, and how to tell friends from strangers. Yet Jimmy showed no interest in Abid'allah: though he was curious about everything, he ignored his mother's best friend. Was he jealous? It didn't seem logical. Perhaps it was simply that the personal chemistry wasn't working.

The whole of Muzeina was surprised by

Olin's transformation. She was more cheerful, and busier, and also on her guard to protect Jimmy from harm. Remember that unlike a mother who belongs to a dolphin pod, she had no nanny available. But the reason why this was striking was because when Abid'allah first got to know her she seemed dumb. This didn't bother him at all, because he was too. But most of the old men believed that the dolphin herself was slightly disabled, and in their view this explained the relationship.

But her baby's presence changed everything. You could hear her speaking to him and whistling his name, and all the sounds audible to human ears were in her mouth. Just like Abid'allah, Olin wasn't dumb after all! Some claimed another miracle, but what was more obvious was that Olin had nothing to say in dolphin speech to humans, no matter how close their friendship.

★   ★   ★

Jimmy twirled around in the small waves of the reef, learning the sea, life, high-speed swimming and even, gradually, acrobatics. He already weighed thirty-three kilos and measured one metre twenty long. Still bearing the pale crease marks of his foetal position, his very supple tail fin was all folded like the fragile leaf of a plant that has grown along a wall. You felt that he was malleable and tender. A handsome baby, he seemed joyful too, and even if the curve of his jawline, so much like a smile, had nothing to do with his mood, it was hard to imagine the youngster being unhappy.

As he grew up, he became more and more curious and fearless. With his mother's permission, he began to play with humans. It was fine proof of the trust and affection that Olin accorded to the Muzeini, and exceptional for any wild animal, but not for Jimmy, who had seen humans since his earliest days — for him they were a feature of the sea, with their flippers and snorkels, their weird cries and especially their laughter. That is what he seemed to enjoy most, and in particular the bursts of laughter from little Ramadan, whom he tried to locate as soon as he sensed his presence with his developing sonar.

Young Ramadan was coming up for ten when I first met him, the glow of his face transected by perfectly even rows of brilliant teeth. A sun child, he simply beamed. He gladdened the eye. He and his friend Falah were mostly in the water, playing, fishing or diving.

When their parents took them away to the

mountains, Ramadan and Falah pined for their new friend. Both have a gift for drawing and an eye for anatomy, and they drew young Jimmy's portrait on the pink granite rocks. They pictured the young dolphin, his fins and bulbous forehead brilliantly observed, in the same way that other tribes paint their divinities. 'Look who we've brought with us!' they seemed to say. 'He's our friend.' I understood them. They have no room with posters on the walls, but at home they have Flipper, in a smaller, wild version. He is not trained to be nice and demonstrative with humans. He is close to those he loves, but doesn't compromise and doesn't seek to entertain anybody but himself. He is a youngster who has quickly shown his sense of independence.

Abid'allah talked about Jimmy with great affection, but though his face lit up it also looked slightly rueful. 'He ignores me, he doesn't like me. When I approach, Olin comes towards me as usual, but he pretends not to see me. I can't touch him: he dodges every time.' Abid'allah was hurt by this indifference. He was like a father who comes home from a long journey to find that his children don't recognize him. All the same, I coaxed him to share with me some of the special childhood moments of the young dolphin who had won the affection of the most resistant Bedouins in Muzeina.

With a spellbound look he told me in Arabic and with expressive signs what a scamp young Jimmy could be. 'You know, he's impulsive, he often defies Olin's whistling. One day he made up his mind to join young Ramadan on the reef.' Already an expert swimmer, Jimmy threaded his way between the outcrops to show himself and earn some caresses from Ramadan, who was overjoyed by this unexpected show of affection. The Bedouins gathered to watch the display. Jimmy was almost on solid ground, in water just a few centimetres deep that lapped across jagged corals. Only his pale stomach and tail were submerged, otherwise his tender skin was exposed to the sun's rays as well as to the stroking of his ecstatic friend. Personally, I see him as trustful: he knows that if he should ground himself by mistake, the humans will float him off again with all the consideration due to his rank as the son of Olin, the queen of Muzeina.

Abid'allah continued his story, grinning as he told it. 'Olin is crazy with worry, and much too big to venture so close to the shore. She knows the dangers for her son, what with the sun on his skin and the razor-edged reef that could do him serious damage. She calls him back, and the little guy hesitates, so pleased with the cuddles and all the attention he's getting from his captive public. So, on our advice, Ramadan and the other children move along with him and lure him out to sea to protect him. Olin gets her son back, and he's sure to have got a good scolding.' He smiles with a glint of affection. 'You see, I'm not always the hero!'

Of all the children in Muzeina, what made Jimmy choose Ramadan? When I ask the question, the good-natured boy is stumped for an answer: it has all come so naturally to him. He has grown up with Olin, and wild dolphins are part of his world, like cows for a child in rural France.

★　★　★

It was dark, and rain was falling.

Safe in his tent, Abid'allah huddled in his burnous. He delighted in the blessing that was drenching the natural world with such fury. He still remembered his childhood, and the storms that frightened him so badly. Twenty years ago ... He could picture himself, a frail child, cradled in the arms of Ahmed Suleiman, Darwish's big brother. He heard the cheerful sound of his mother's footsteps, she was so lively and so steadfast

. . . He felt lulled by the last winter rains, as sweet as love. With Muhammad and Juma, he used to share a bachelors' tent. They ate as a family, their meals prepared by aunts or female cousins, except for the fresh fish that they grilled for themselves on the beach. An icy southern breeze enveloped their *kitoun*. The concave shapes of mountains brushed in kohl were bathing under cloudy moonlight. Abid'allah was jolted out of his daydreams by a serious uproar outside. Neighbours rushed into the tent, taking the three friends by surprise. 'Olin, Olin,' they shouted, 'we can't see her, we don't know what's happening. Come and see.'

Abid'allah had already put his sandals on. He was followed outside helter-skelter by Juma and Muhammad, who had understood nothing in the gloom of the tent. Nor had Abid'allah, but he had heard their panic, with Olin's name involved, and that was enough to make him run as fast as he could. These three friends are not men of the word, but all their deeds come from the heart.

Olin was shrieking in desperation. Under the driving rain, they tried to locate her, the boat's engine echoing in the depths. Olin's cries were rending Abid'allah's heart, yet he couldn't tell what could be causing such distress. Then there was no time for questions: there she was. Muhammad and Abid'allah dived in together, not stopping to confer.

They soon understood when they followed her in the moonlight at shallow depth. Jimmy was tangled up in some ropes, and there was nothing Olin could do by herself to free him from this deadly trap. He was still alive, but hardly stirring, stuck fast and petrified, and out of air. The two men pulled at the ropes, but it was going to take a knife, and neither had one. The dolphin calf had minutes left to live. So mustering all their strength, they tore at the rope, picking it apart in shreds and handfuls, in an attempt to slowly tease him free. It worked.

Watched by his desperate mother, they brought the little body up to the surface and straight into the boat, where Abid'allah breathed into his blowhole, giving the child the kiss of life. He breathed into him all the air he could, as hard as he could, and Jimmy revived. Soon he was breathing, softly, on his own. His liquid eyes seemed to be thanking his rescuers, a look so touching that Muhammad and Abid'allah were never to forget it.

After a few minutes they decided to try to return the dolphin to the sea. Abid'allah panted for breath, and the downpour washed away the salt that stung the wounds in their bleeding hands, and they felt glad. Olin was silent, and stuck close to the pitching, creaking boat. To this day, you can see the scars from the rope cuts in Muhammad's right palm. Once more the Bedouins of Muzeina had saved a dolphin's life.

* * *

The sun reappeared from behind its screen of cloud. After the rain, the tattered village opened a new eye. The smells of earth and iodine merged, and placed the men on a bridge between their desert and their sea. Then they had to sort out the priorities: either bale out the boats and clean up the beach, or else wait for the sun and set off into the mountains, where the family elders were staying, together with most of the women and their youngest children.

When he woke up, Abid'allah went to join Olin. For the first time, Jimmy arrived before his mother, rubbed his snout against Abid'allah's shoulder, and stopped still, his rostrum nuzzling Abid'allah's neck. Abid'allah felt a bit nervous about this sudden show of affection from the toddler. But after all, last night he had saved his life . . . and this gratitude melted him. So strong was his emotion at this that he hardly breathed a word about it in the village. He, the natural show-off, contented himself with saying that at long last, Jimmy loved him too — loved his father Abid'allah.

Olin's Muzeina

Nuweiba el Muzeina,
feast of Aïd-el-Kebir, 1997

At the request of old Mekhassen, the children scampered from house to house to summon all the wise men. On the agenda was the question of the new revenue linked to the dolphin, for that morning Abid'allah had asked a group of six German tourists to pay ten Egyptian pounds each (about one pound fifty sterling) to go swimming with Olin in the bay. His father was determined to avoid a scandal, so before the rumour spread he asked for a meeting on the subject.

Abid'allah heard the news like all the other inhabitants, and he was hopping mad, but he had no power to reverse the rulings of the elders, who embarked on a broad debate about the subject. Ibrahim the egghead spoke first, and he explored the questions that needed to be asked: 'Is it right to make the tourists pay so as to make a profit out of Olin? How much should they be charged?' Assuming a casual tone, he added: 'But most of all ... who does the money go to?' And there the debate could have turned sour. In fact, they were all more or less agreed about cashing in on the dolphin's services. The tourists benefited from her, so it was natural for them to contribute to the costs. But, in Ibrahim's words: 'If you are eating, why shouldn't I eat too?' They all wanted their slice of the cake.

At that point Abid'allah intervened. Standing in a corner of the circle, with one foot on the pipe of a spluttering hookah, he warned: 'Olin is mine. It's for my sake that she stays in Muzeina, and if you stop me from earning my living, then I will leave with her, and go a long way from here.' One by one, he stared them in the eye, to make sure of having been heard, him and his threat. Then in a flash, the way he came, he headed for the sea again, under the noses of the wise men, who were obliged to take the boy's wishes into account. His father, old Mekhassen, kept quiet.

Nearly all the families of the Nuweiba el Muzeina clan have owned their patch of this beach for several generations. It has been divided up for centuries, one and a half kilometres of barren, useless land that nobody cared about before the miracles, and the coming of the dolphin.

It was up to the sheikh to conclude. 'Young Mekhassen has a point. The dolphin obeys

188

him, he's the one who mostly looks after her, so he should receive at least half. We'll share out the rest according to who owns the land on the beach. Whoever has a plot there gets a share.' So it was decided that the old people would take turns to guard the access to the beach, and charge ten guineas to any adult who wanted to swim near the dolphin. They all went home, feeling quite nervous. This new collective economic activity was nothing like the traditional fishing, herding, or growing dates and olives. At best, it would take time for the clan to digest it all and get organized. Having a maverick like Abid'allah Mekhassen at the heart of the problem didn't make things any easier. But not a word would be spoken against him. Nowadays, everyone respects him: his special talents have earned him the status of a wise man. He is seen as one of the pillars of Muzeina.

Madane laughs heartily when Ibrahim recalls that famous meeting and the family disputes to settle who gets what. In his immaculate Hebrew, he stresses: 'Pascale, have you ever heard of an animal transforming a whole society? Isn't that crazy? Even in Israel, you've never seen anything like it. Not even in Europe, I'll bet! Do you personally know anybody silly enough to let a fish — all right, a big fish — decide their future? I didn't believe it was possible, but it's happening where I live, right where I live!'

*   *   *

All those who meet her are tempted to project on to Olin their fears, desires, and inner thoughts. There she is, both present and absent at the same time. Mostly, she co-operates — sometimes without a breath of movement. She 'stands' up straight in front of Abid'allah or Muhammad, with all her power contained, focused on stillness. They coax and hug and laugh, and she stays poised and stoical, till the moment comes when she darts away, pulling her playmate behind her. Then she suddenly turns on her back, offering her speckled belly to be fondled. She loves the attention of her true friends, those she has known for some time, and swims very slowly, to enable them to follow. The proof is that when Abid'allah enters the water she races towards him and pulls him out to sea at top speed, because she knows what a brilliant diver he is: no danger of his getting lost en route!

Oz and the friends from Dolphin Reef are positive. Olin is in perfect health, she can reach a swimming speed of twenty kilometres an hour, like all ambassador dolphins. But because she is careful about contact with the humans who come to see her, she lives at a slower tempo with them. When she goes out to sea, out of our sight, she must let rip, and leap and plunge even more than she does with Abid'allah!

Oz also says that she is especially strong, because she faces the predators that are bound to threaten Jimmy on her own, and easily sees them off.

Today, worldwide, there are about thirteen male and female dolphins, all of the species Tursiops, that are practically settled and in regular contact with humans. Not one of them is dependent on humans to eat: if they take food, it is in play or out of affection.

Contrary to what has often been claimed, these ambassadors usually keep in touch with their original school, and are not outcasts. But according to the Australian cetologist Michael Bossley, all these individuals have suffered some grave trauma in the past, and are seeking a limited security zone around some landmark object — a boat or a buoy, for example — and often around a strong bond of friendship. That is the case with Olin: since her arrival in Muzeina, thin, visibly in shock, and lonely after her companion's death, in a way she has woven her own net. She has drawn a line from one shore to the other of the lagoon, a psychological frontier on the Muzeina reef, where she feels on home territory and which separates her from the rest of the Red Sea. She has chosen to live her daily life and make her haven in a narrow area of about four thousand square metres. Of all the dolphins directly involved with humans, it seems that only Olin has chosen such a small habitat, and only she has a special friend whom she strongly prefers to any other swimming partner.

More and more tourists are flocking to Muzeina. Mostly the village is quiet, and then come the school holidays in Israel, or Christmas in Europe, and whole minibuses are unloading their cargo on the beach. It is striking to see how at one moment the bay can be invaded by laughter and cheerful shouting in a blend of Italian and English, and the next minute brings a chorus of Swedish. While their voices mingle on the sand, their eyes look seawards, where the dolphin rides.

With the help of the Egyptian guides, the Bedouins on the beach have to watch the swimmers' activities, but most of all they have to protect Olin, who gets nervous and uncomfortable with more than twenty people in the water. When the bathers visit Olin in just small groups, then she will graciously share her lagoon and receive her guests.

I have often wondered how she can stand these intrusions and not show a trace of irritation. In her place I would be out to sea till the invasion eased off. Of course, when the tourists are not really welcome she keeps her distance, or swims a few metres down, too deep for most swimmers who can't dive. But she always stays in sight: everybody gets to enjoy the lines of her body and dolphin smile. Is she 'hooked' on humans, or is she so keen to please Abid'allah that she has grown psychologically dependent? Does she approach people for her own sake, or has she got a tacit agreement with Abid'allah: that to please him, she has to please the rest?

According to Oz Goffman, her key role in the lagoon enables her to handle all this fuss without stress. The men in her new clan, King Abid'allah, who represents the alpha male, the one who brings her affection, the personal bond she needs, the friend Muhammad, and Juma the court jester, are all at her beck and call. And all who enter her living space are governed by the laws of her friends, laws that are probably more or less ones she has introduced herself, in the course of their relationship together. She is the queen in her domain, which is undoubtedly matriarchal.

Yet dolphins are no angels, and if anything

are closer to men, with their faults and virtues, their intelligence, and sometimes their barbarities. We often forget to mention their distressing behaviour, when, alone or in schools, they chase and violate females, or sometimes murder their own kind. The myth that surrounds them is illusory. They can certainly be jealous or hostile, even manipulative, in order to keep their status in the clan. They each have their own specific character, and that is what makes them truly attractive. How do you develop a relationship with an object, no matter how superb? Every dolphin has a soul, a personality, and Olin proves it every day with her helpfulness and indifference, her fidelity and her jealousy.

★　★　★

The Egyptian navy keeps a presence on the coasts of the Red Sea. The coast guards' routine work is to keep a lookout for illegal fishing, smuggling and various other offences. Sometimes, when something intrigues them, or maybe lured by pretty tourists swimming, they call at Nuweiba el Muzeina, where they are always made welcome, because it's in the locals' interests, and traditional hospitality requires it.

In March 1997, a buzz was going round,

and the men were edgy, both on shore and out at sea. The patrol boats were angling shoreward, and the Muzeini were in a flap. Was this a cautionary exercise, or had the Bedouins been fishing in a grey area? Olin was very upset by all this uproar. She cruised her reef from north to south and then from south to north, not knowing how to protect her territory, her offspring, her life. Her beach had already been invaded by raucous Martians — a group of about ten Italian tourists splashing on the reef, laughing and joshing one another, the girls curvaceous in their bright yellow bikinis, the men in long shorts, all larking about in the sky-blue sea, oblivious of other people, or the rumpus the navy were making. For Olin, this din was only adding to her confusion. Why were these people so cheerful when all her friends were nervy, and these noisy little ships were invading her waters? Unfortunately, Abid'allah had gone fishing out at sea, and of those who perceived the dolphin's distress, nobody knew how to help. Dolphins are jeopardized by panic; it can kill them. Some that have been found drowned in caves or caught in nets have not died of wounds or any concrete medical cause. Their hearts have stopped because their hypersensitivity makes them utterly vulnerable to many kinds of stress.

Julia was one of those pacing up and down on the beach. With her little round spectacles and serious air, this Hungarian physiotherapist is one of the courtiers, the Western lovers who come to swim with Olin for several months of the year. She didn't know what to do. Finally she decided to dive in to reassure her dolphin friend. I'm human, after all, she thought, it's my duty to protect her from the other intruders of my species. She donned her mask and snorkel, and dived in to join Olin, stroking her fin to calm her, and trying to lead her away, to a safer distance from the snarl of the circling engines and the tension of the Bedouins. But Olin remained afraid, Jimmy huddled up against her.

Julia, convinced that she had to help, pushed her seaward, but without success. Olin opened her jaws and bared her sharp teeth, which Julia took as a sign of gratitude, and she continued to stroke her, lean on her, and heave with all her strength. But Olin is far stronger than a young woman, and more than that, she was in her element. Julia, with all her thoughts of rescue, was in more ways than one out of her depth. Olin is a dolphin at large, a wild animal, and Julia had forgotten that. As a motorboat's sharp propeller passed a few metres away from them, Olin's patience snapped. She bit at Julia, who pulled her hand away in a panic.

Julia was horrified. Olin had bitten the little finger of her left hand, and severed the last two joints. Defeated and shocked, she swam slowly to shore, her hand gushing blood. A friend with a first-aid kit cleaned the wound with iodine and bandaged her finger with compresses, and Julia sat on a wall and stared at her idol's dorsal fin puzzling at what had got into her.

Next day, Julia was feeling better. She explained to everybody: 'Olin mistook me for another dolphin, because we're very close. Dolphins bite each other, she thought I was challenging her status as top dolphin in Muzeina.' She smiled, and looked genuinely glad. 'I should be proud that my friend took me for another dolphin . . . ' But the others, her foreign friends and the Bedouins, were worried. 'How are you going to be able to give massages like that?' Julia didn't know.

Next day, all was quiet in Muzeina. Waves lapped against the pebbles that gleamed at the foot of the beach, and formed little pools for the toddlers' pleasure. Julia's finger was dangerously swollen, so she was taken to hospital, a few hundred kilometres away. As far as I know she has never returned to Muzeina. I heard that she fell in love with her

Egyptian doctor in hospital, converted to Islam and married him, and that she is living happily with him in Alexandria . . .

★ ★ ★

As Juma, Muhammad and Abid'allah sit cross-legged beside me, I ask in my stumbling sign language what they think about this bad experience of Julia's. I'm halfway through my question when Muhammad bursts out: 'You too? Do you realize what you're saying? Julia was an accident, she tried to use force on Olin.' He says it again: 'USE FORCE.' Juma breaks in with a hand on his shoulder: 'He gets upset because of the newspaper reports that told the story and claimed it proved that Olin was aggressive and dangerous.' Silence falls. Coffee is served, with a kick like a mule. Muhammad calms down and resumes his explanation: 'You know, she's delicate in her way, I can understand how she sometimes gets bad-tempered. You don't approach a wild dolphin any way you please — not Olin, anyway,' he corrects himself, not knowing any other dolphins. He may have passed by schools of them at sea, but they rarely collect around boats for long enough to let themselves be approached.

I ask the three friends for instructions on

first meeting a dolphin, taking out my pencil and battered notebook, a cue that they take very seriously.

Juma, Abid'allah and Muhammad look at each other, then Abid'allah begins: 'Olin has friends. Tourists are passing strangers, and for her that's very different. Some people come here to see her, and forget that she is just as much to be respected as a human being: they want to touch her, poke their fingers in her blowhole, and hang on to her fin.' He stands up and raises his voice: 'Pascale, imagine, I enter your house, just like that, I touch you, I stick my fingers up your nose, and I grab you if you act as if you're leaving! Imagine that!' I burst out laughing, because he's enhancing his account with sign language, and I can visualize the scene. 'No, no . . . it isn't funny. If anyone acts that way with me, he gets a punch in the nose! Olin is very patient, but really she's like everybody else — she has her limits.' I myself have heard stories of dolphins injuring people who make a nuisance of themselves.

The extreme case is the dolphin called Tiao, in Brazil, who damaged several people with blows from his flukes, including a drunken man who died of his injuries some hours later. Apparently these people had been really mistreating him, and in self-defence he smacked his attackers hard in the stomach. That was in 1994, and since then no other incident has been reported. Tiao is living happily on the coast, sometimes mixing with humans, and is protected by an association.

No cetacean has ever attacked a man except in a case of genuine self-defence or in a context of utter panic. But dolphins can be jealous of their best friends or of their conquests.

I tell this story to Abid'allah, who takes up the subject. 'Yes, Olin has fits of jealousy with me too!' Quite glad to hear that this happens with many other dolphins, he tells me about Asher's daughter's unhappy experience. When she was very young, she went over to the reef when Abid'allah was dishing out a ration of caresses to his dolphin. Without warning, the dolphin swooped at her, giving her a smack on the head with her tail-fin. 'She was bleeding . . . but luckily it wasn't serious,' Abid'allah insists, looking uneasy all the same. Another young woman had a finger bone torn off by Olin, who was jealous of the woman's privileged relationship with Abid'allah.

Stung once again, Muhammad intervenes: 'That's true, but you've really got to know her to touch her, and thousands of people have spent time with her without anything happening to them at all. And especially now, Abid'allah knows about her jealousy and its effects, and acts accordingly.' In another life, Muhammad was probably a lawyer.

Juma, very much the practical member of the gang, gives me a tap on the shoulder. He signs to me: 'Now the instructions for swimming with Olin.' He is standing up to give the demonstration in sign language: 'One: you put on flippers or sandals, because the reef is sharp in places. Two: you bring a mask and snorkel, so as to be comfortable with your head under water. Three: you don't rush it.' I ask for a break, because in order to follow his account I am obliged to look at Juma, who speaks in nothing but incoherent onomatopoeic grunts, then look at my notebook to write, and my giggles don't make the job easier. Muhammad and Abid'allah are doubled up with laughter, and the leader takes advantage of the interval to go and order tea from his cousin. We start again. 'So. Three: don't rush. Four: you enter the water where it's deeper and look out for Olin (he signs 'binoculars') without swerving right or left. Watch out, you're in her space. Five: she arrives, and you swim with your hands folded over your stomach or behind your back, to signal, basically, I'm not one of these idiots who go rushing straight at you for no reason. Six, the best way to get her feeling very curious is to make a distinctive noise like banging two stones together, or calling or singing. Seven: second trick, all by yourself, play some seemingly fascinating game, and she'll be tempted to come and see what's happening and play along with you.'

I laugh a lot at Juma's humour. It seems to me that he has served up his own brand of personal experience combined with what the dolphin lovers have read in the textbooks. Having said that, I have already used this procedure in the water with Olin. I've even played with an old car tyre for ten minutes to lure her to come and join me, but without success!

Nature boy

Nuweiba el Muzeina, April 1997

Shopping duty at the little village grocery. We walk on the blend of sand and beaten earth in the village streets, past the forecourts of houses where the sound of bickering alternates with women's laughter. Long-haired goats and a few young dromedaries graze peacefully, and scavenge the unseen vegetation that lurks between the stones.

Something remarkable is going on under my eyes: every dog we meet comes over to greet Abid'allah. Through concentrating on my friends' conversation, I failed to notice at first, but after a few metres it gets impossible to ignore: as if they were paying respects, these animals are sidling up to Abid'allah and poking their noses into his hand. He keeps on walking and talking, but the dogs trot up to him, nuzzle him one by one, then go about their business. No one seems to notice this marvel. No animal approaches me, or Darwish, or his elder son. Only Abid'allah enjoys this amazing attention. In two streets, how many stray dogs have greeted him? I

203

interrupt his conversation: 'Abid'allah, the dogs here seem very fond of you . . . '

'Yes, I suppose they do. It's always been like that with animals, you know.'

I'm beginning to understand. This man has a true gift for communicating with animals. A very particular gift, and hard to sum up in a word, something inside him, an aspect of character that domestic and wild animals recognize, and we do not . . .

Next day I ask Abid'allah to take me out fishing with him. Oh, of course I won't be much use, but I'm curious to find out how he regularly brings back a bigger catch than the other Bedouins.

Five in the morning, and I wake up first. I put on my swimsuit, always ready at the foot of my sleeping bag, and go down to the reef. Without Juma's cushions under my bottom, I proceed with caution, because there's a risk of being stung by the dorsal spine of a stonefish. You have to look out for these invisible, perfectly camouflaged fishes whose venom can be lethal. Although in popular mythology it is sharks you have to fear, in practice it is these drab little predators that are the real threat on the Red Sea reefs. So as I advance I keep my eyes glued to the jagged surface just beneath the water, and as soon as I have clearance I stretch out and swim, with my body pleasurably suspended over the danger, and over the corals whose colours appear once you reach a few metres off shore. Olin is not far away — I can see her dorsal fin behind the two boats moored near the beach, and occasionally Jimmy's smaller fin beside her.

Once I am out in the water, which is warm as usual, with almost no effort I head towards them. I never know what dolphins really see. We have our subjective, human impressions, our projections and fantasies . . . but it's a mystery. Olin is at arm's length from my shoulder, no more and no less, but she does not come close. I think I understand that she is still testing me, but maybe this is just the distance that suits her.

Suddenly I found myself thinking about Flipper, and about Ric O'Barry, his trainer. Flipper the dolphin, the hero of the American TV series of the 1970s, was played in succession by six male and female dolphins. Between Ric and the last dolphin, Kathy, a friendship developed, and in the end Ric realized that she was unhappy in captivity. He couldn't bear his work any longer, and resigned from the Miami Seaquarium. Later, Kathy fell ill in her concrete pool, and they sent for her friend Ric. The moment he entered the water, she slipped into his arms and breathed her final breath. She seems to have waited to die until he came. Ric O'Barry was shattered by what happened, and threw himself passionately into the fight against the capture and captivity of dolphins. He campaigned against the army using dolphins to place mines on submarines and the dolphinariums, and tried time after time to 'free' dolphins into the wild after 'rehabilitating' them. But it doesn't work in reverse, the reintroductions failed. It seems that once a dolphin has adapted to captivity, it cannot re-adapt to the wild.

Facing Olin, the queen of Muzeina, I felt like bringing him here, so that he could see this reality, this dolphin who has trained men to respect, love and understand her. Yet another lesson for me, and not the last.

★ ★ ★

Lost in my thoughts, and watching Olin and her son swim in waters that shone turquoise in the morning light, I failed to see Abid'allah arriving, but she spotted him at once. I hung back, to savour the sunrise scene. Jimmy flitted joyfully around them, Olin absorbed her friend's caresses with transparent delight. They went racing towards the open sea, while I returned to the beach. Looking out, you could catch sight of a sudden flurry, and sometimes three heads that surfaced to breathe and then instantly submerged. I was smiling. Whereas when I am close to Olin I'm a spectator, busy musing and admiring, Abid'allah finds in her his best friend, and a dynamic, powerful interchange like nothing else I know of. Surprisingly, I felt a little empty, but soon Darwish, and then the two inseparables, Ibrahim and Madane, arrived to greet me. I myself would not replace these human friends for anything in the world.

Ibrahim pointed at my wet T-shirt: 'Aha! You've been with 'amazing'!' I didn't get it. He repeated: 'That's it, 'amazing'.' They were joking, and Darwish, who hadn't understood, requested a translation in sign language and burst out laughing when he got one. I know what 'amazing' means in English, but I didn't see the connection, if any, with my going swimming ... 'Sure,' said Madane, with his usual quizzical look, 'all the foreigners say that when they come out of the water, 'Amazing, amazing' — about the dolphin.' At last I got it. They were making fun of the tourists' sense of wonder when faced with a creature that the boys had been meeting every day for years. Ibrahim caught my eye, to ask me: 'Do you know what 'amazing' means?' I told him, and we all laughed out loud, because none of them had thought of such a simple meaning. To them, it had to stand for something immense and mysterious, since these visitors seemed so happy.

With the influx of Western tourists, the Bedouins have discovered the international language — English. Even the oldest of them want to know the meaning of various words, like Ahmed's and Darwish's father, ninety years old at least, who asked me one morning how to say 'welcome' in the tourists' language. To him, all Westerners have the same mother tongue, because he only hears them speak to his sons in English.

★ ★ ★

Abid'allah came back for his milky morning coffee. Deep in thought, and looking very serious, he announced: 'We must go fishing straight away.' He already knew where he was bound. What had he seen? Maybe Olin had told him what was good on that day's menu? In any case I was ready, which was just as well, since he doesn't wait for anybody.

The clean nets, the fish-hooks, the pick-up truck. I was surprised by Abid'allah's sense of organization and team leadership . . . it's unusual for Bedouins to hurry like that. 'Let's go! To work, to work!' he shouted, with one finger on his diver's watch.

The sun was still tender, pink and mild. Abid'allah scanned the open sea, sticking his head through the window. 'There!' and he pointed to a spot on the horizon. I could see nothing special on the surface of the sea, no birds in the sky, no stain on the water . . . but my friend was too focused to answer my questions. I'd soon see. In fact I will never know, and nor will anybody else, how he chooses his fishing grounds.

We stopped, and the men and children entered the water to place the nets about eight metres down on the edge of the coral banks. Then we continued to cruise along the coast. At the moment when Abid'allah called out and levelled an outstretched arm at a point that no one can see, we changed our course for the beach, and more nets were set. After two or three hours we covered the coast in the opposite direction to retrieve the nets and the catch. Abid'allah wanted to catch a shoal of *rim*, those beautiful blue fish whose French name I don't know, but it would have to wait.

Inspecting the nets, we found many small fish from the reef had been caught. The sunlight glittered on their scales as they kept on wriggling in the baskets. Red mullet, stellate rabbitfish, rainbow wrasse, small pipefish ... Turquoise, red, bright yellow ... all the colours in the world, dying in their wickerwork prisons. But surprisingly, the sight was not a sad one. I knew that they would be eaten with relish by the beautiful children of Muzeina, or that they would act as bait for other, bigger, more expensive fish that would be sold on the market in Nuweiba or Dahab to buy clothing, meat or medicines. The colours of the sea feed Muzeina.

In the past, fishing was only a supplement, and fish were caught to be dried and salted for winter-time, or eaten fresh at home. Today the Muzeini do not migrate with their herds as much as they used to, and the price of the bigger fish has shot up, boosted by foreign demand. So it is profitable to sell them, and for the Muzeini to exploit their skills as fishermen. Abid'allah is well informed about all this, having started to fish as soon as Darwish taught him to swim, before his seventh birthday. Darwish himself does not know how to fish, and Abid'allah has never taught him, but sometimes he supplies his elder brother — I have seen him choose the fish as he empties the baskets.

That day, the fishing was not yet over. Abid'allah set out again in the newly repainted boat, always turquoise blue for luck and by preference. He took his lines and, with two boys helping him, put out bait in the hope of catching some of the big groupers that spawn in the Red Sea's waters.

The engine revved, and its backwash seemed to make fun for Olin and Jimmy, who followed in the wake and revelled in their travelling jacuzzi. We were far out to sea, a new desert of blue, black and grey. The lines were promising, and the bow pitched above the deep, a thousand metres of life and strange noises below us. Abid'allah was on the alert. He looked like a primitive hunter, lying in wait for the slightest sign of the prey that he knows at first hand.

The nature that surrounds Abid'allah Mekhassen meshes with his own. It is at sea that he feels most himself. From the surface, he sees the life that spreads beneath the waves. To say that Abid'allah is an exceptional diver and fisherman is true, but it goes much further than that. For years, the sea was his only refuge, both his school and his home. When Olin arrived, maybe she taught him her ruthless hunter's tricks. As catchers of fish, dolphins are infallible: they are among the greatest ocean predators. Even if Abid'allah lacks their tools of sonar and hearing, he senses the sea, and especially its fauna, the fish, squid and cetaceans. In himself, he is a bridge between animals and other men. For me, as I watched him in his boat, merging with the sea spray, it seemed perhaps his deafness that sensitized him so particularly — to Olin's body language, of course, but long before that to the language of fish and their movements. Why does he catch them so much more easily, always knowing where to find them in the vastness of the sea?

It is not only Abid'allah's exceptional eyes but also his whole body that tracks down his prey. Standing in the bow, his torso and the palms of his hands were bunched with the strain of waiting, and his shoulders defied the gusting north wind. Suddenly his arm was as tense as a bowstring, pointing south-eastward. Without a word, the two boys weighed anchor and rowed calmly in that direction.

What had he sensed? A school of fish, less than a kilometre, possibly four hundred metres away. The anchor dropped and caught on a rock, perhaps some extremely rare coral . . . The lines twitched, it seemed that the fish were biting, and soon the floor of the boat was strewn with big tuna, barracuda and grouper, each of them over a kilo. I was surrounded by masses of muscle, still hopelessly writhing. The grim, almost sinister look on Abid'allah's face dissolved in my wide-eyed stare, and slowly the familiar proud smile re-emerged. I offered the palm of my hand for him to slap. 'Not bad, right?' He shrugged his shoulders, obviously pleased to have proved his skill, not to mention earned his day's keep. He kissed the sky with his fingertips, and I translated out loud: '*Min Allah!*'

Olin uttered shrill little cries to attract his attention. She knew that the work was done.

The lines were piled up on the thwarts and the two boys skylarked around. Abid'allah looked at me, as if to say: 'Can I help it if she loves me?' then dived overboard the way the rest of us would step off a pavement, with the ease of familiar practice. I leaned out over the side, with my hands and hair in the water, to cool down. Suddenly Jimmy was pointing his snout at me, his rostrum touching my forehead. It felt as if he was saying, 'I want a friend to play with too . . . ' I melted. He was cuter even than Olin, so sweet and innocent, like a kitten or a bear cub.

He bobbed up still further out of the water and stretched towards me while I stroked his throat. His skin had a texture hard to describe. Soviet scientists in the Cold War era tried, but failed, to produce a synthetic equivalent. Its aerodynamic efficiency in water is unequalled on our planet. He dipped beneath the boat again, to return to his mother I suppose, because I know she hates him going close to strangers. She must have whistled his name under the water.

The sea looked beautiful. That simple greeting from Jimmy filled me with a strange sense of bliss, a kind of fullness that flooded me with positive energy. And this is the dolphin's primary gift to humans. It is much more than good humour, it is happiness in doses.

Changes at Muzeina

Muzeina beach, Easter 1997

Martin is a thirty-five-year-old actor from London. Sitting cross-legged in front of me, with a keffiyeh wrapped round his forehead and a blissful smile creasing his freckled face, he tells me what he does in Muzeina for six months of the year. 'One night five years ago I was by myself in my flat and I had a dream that has permanently changed me. I saw a marvellous bottlenose dolphin, we swam together, and danced in the waves, and he threw a new light on my life.' Quite soon, in New Age circles in England, from dolphin lovers and meditation adepts, he heard talk of a female dolphin loose in the Red Sea, and linked her with his favourable vision. He decided to go and see for himself, not knowing how true the rumours were, and after some searching around he discovered Muzeina. First he fell in love with Olin, then with the Bedouins, and last year with a young Israeli diver who has given him a child.

He comes several times a year to retrieve the reality of his vision. Altogether, he has already spent almost three years here. To finance his journeys, each time he comes Martin escorts a small group of English people to see Olin and the Sinai. These unusual tourists come to meditate, discover themselves, and strengthen their relationship with nature. They are men and women who are seeking to rebuild their lives in a different way. They have a quest. A spiritual, personal quest, which is not always easy to understand for those who do not share it.

They say that they are seeking well-being and a kind of inner truth, by way of music, reading, yoga and other exercises. They study the Bible, and great mystic writers such as Rumi. Some have become Buddhists. At first these puzzled the Bedouins. Unlike the Israeli hippies and conventional tourists, they need seclusion, and their great feasts round the bonfire, when tea takes the place of alcohol, came as a surprise. Martin himself is very much at ease. He tells his own versions of Bedouin legends, with his actor's skill and perfect English diction. He has learned how not to leave his dream behind.

Then there is Helen, his compatriot, who trails her sandals by the water's edge. With her head reaching out to the infinite blue sky, she seems never to touch the sand with her hands, but only to skim over it, never to speak to anyone, but to imagine them. She has no dream, but simply a quest. All year long, Helen deals with her many responsibilities near Oxford, and she uses her holidays to slip away to Muzeina. Every day she swims close to Olin, and she mentions her with love: 'Being with Olin opens my whole body, and takes all my pressures away. They say that the sound of their sonar, which we only partly hear, affects us and makes our brain produce alpha waves, the sign of relaxation. Anyway, it works for me. I feel happy all the time here, thanks to her. I feel free.'

Helen seems delighted to share her experience with me. The Bedouins view her as some sort of crank. Only Juma is truly friends with her. 'He's teaching me sign language, and we talk for hours, we walk by the seaside, and I forget all about my everyday life, so grey in England!' In her multicoloured cotton trousers and XXL T-shirt, she is attached to this place, where she has a hut and her personal routines; she feels at home, a slightly imaginary second home, standing on the shore of the Red Sea, where the girls braid her hair and make new bracelets for her every day.

Like dozens of others, here Martin and Helen have found an essential complement to their daily lives. Far from the classic stop-off

— a few hours' stay, a quick look at Olin and the Bedouins — these tourists are almost on home ground here. I say almost because the Muzeini obviously do not incorporate them in their clan. They remain strangers, even if their sense of belonging anchors them deep in this decidedly pluralist place. It seems that nobody can ever become a Bedouin.

In the Sinai desert the elements touch without ever fusing or being part of one another. The essence of each thing seems unchanging. The Bedouin is the Bedouin, the woman is different from the man, the mountains never yield to the traveller, though the traveller can shelter among their rocks. The dromedary belongs to the wise Bedouin who knows how to treat it. The well and fresh water belong, like everything else, to Allah, whose wishes are men's wishes. Each component of the desert — human, vegetable or mineral — has its place. To seek to change that order could bring nothing but destruction.

Muzeina beach, May 1997

Of the ten Egyptian pounds that he earns from admissions to the beach, Abid'allah seems to spend it all from day to day. He pays to hire the Jeep and equipment to go fishing, and for various people's services. He lends money when he is asked, and hands out loose change to elated local children.

Yet, next to his stone cabin, the pioneer venture on this once deserted beach, Abid'allah decided that he must have a hotel. He paid another visit to the nearby town of Dahab, found an Egyptian *mouhendis*, a construction engineer, and persuaded him to come and inspect the site and assess the work required. Abid'allah put a payment down straight away, because he was in a hurry, and wanted to provide a service for the growing number of tourists. He wanted two storeys, alcove windows, and a terrace to overlook the sea. He wanted lots of concrete, plus modern tiling later, for the walls and floors. He had the cash to get started — and so he presented the *mouhendis*, slightly surprised by this peculiarly talkative Bedouin, with wads of Egyptian banknotes tied up with string.

By the following week, the men were already at work. The Egyptian architect was familiar enough with local customs to know that it's best to start as soon as possible, before the money runs out in overheads and various rakeoffs. The work got going, Egyptian style: two builders dig, another three watch or keep them supplied, then they swap round.

As Abid'allah walked about in the village, dressed in a full-length white jellaba and looking straight ahead from under his traditional keffiyeh, everyone greeted him and asked after his health, as tradition demands. And each of them looked hard at him. In practice he has become the young sheikh of the village, a leader and public figure. It is a rare foreigner who does not inquire about *Abdallah*, as they call him, before he puts his bags down. For good and all, fame has made him a man of influence.

When his mood seems good — the Arab proverb says '*Yom Assal, Yom Bassal*', one day honey, next day onions — children come to him looking for pocket money, and old or needy people with families hard up for cash also simply ask, because for him it is a great pleasure: being able to be generous is the clinching sign of his success. I would say that he has become the 'Godfather' of Muzeina, because his wishes tend to be granted. For example, Abid'allah Mekhassen is the only Muzeini to have been issued with a passport by the Sinai prefecture, even though he had to pay through the nose and wait for months to be allowed to leave the area.

When he wanted electricity installed in his

220

hotel, the public electricity company that supplies the beach agreed in exchange for a sizeable bribe. A first. But it seems that he will be the only one to score such a victory.

* * *

For inhabitants, the Sinai laws are a total block on freedom. I realized this once again on the occasion of a visit to my friend Fatma, the healer. Her husband, Darwish, asked to take me there so that he could try out my car. It didn't matter to him that the house was only a few metres away. Darwish loves driving. That was his job with Asher for some time, but now it is totally forbidden. He explained to me that the Egyptian government has withdrawn the driving licences from all disabled people, whatever their problem is. No deaf person in Muzeina can now borrow a vehicle to chauffeur tourists, or work on tractors, as they used to do. What an injustice! Darwish added: 'That's why we're poor today — me and my eight children: I can't work any more, the way I used to.' He drove with such pleasure! He felt the engine purring by its vibrations, and congratulated me: 'Great car! May Allah guard you!' The children had already rushed off to warn the mistress of the house, and I lent the vehicle to Darwish for an hour, telling him that I didn't give a hoot for such stupid laws, and that I would see to everything if there was any trouble — implying that I would pay the necessary bribe to get him released if the police picked him up.

Darwish's second cousin was there, a tall, diffident woman, sitting waiting in a corner of the courtyard. With her sad and constantly drooping face, she seemed to embody a swamp or quicksand, in which she was stuck. In the West, we would call her depressed; for the Bedouins she is sick or bewitched, and only a healer can help her. Fatma the *dotora* has succeeded her mother in this ancestral craft.

In the patio, the children romped, and I talked to the young women about marriage and family. The sun still blazed, though it was late afternoon. Fatma got things ready. A charcoal fire and incense. A basin of water, and handfuls of coarse salt. In the corner of the yard where she had been sitting on bare concrete for half an hour, the cousin lay down quietly on her side, wrapped in her robes and veils, as if to die. All I could see was her back, but I guessed that her eyes were closed on her painful inner world. Fatma knelt beside her, with her right fist clenched round a handful of coarse salt.

She concentrated, and her otherwise

cheerful face tensed. She passed her fist over her patient's body, from head to foot, and over her hips and stomach. The pain in this woman flowed through Fatma, who started and whimpered, chanted and moaned. No loud cries or big gestures, the two women united around the same pain. Minutes crawled by, then Fatma opened her eyes and fist, and a little of her body, to stand up. Her cousin followed, and they both sat ceremoniously by the fire, which they fed with twigs. Release had yet to come. I sensed the extreme tension that bound them both to another place I did not wish to enter. Their two faces were painful to watch.

Reciting what I took for a prayer, the *dotora* threw the salt into the fire. It had absorbed the sickness and must be purified. Then the cousin stood, and Fatma, squatting beside her, slid the bowl of incense and embers underneath her skirts. The smoke rose, and emerged at her neck, which was suddenly more relaxed. She was almost smiling. The intense heat engrossed her body for some minutes.

That was it. The cousin took her leave, with a faint nod of her head in my direction and then towards the girls. I felt moved, and Fatma understood. She was visibly tired, but she sat with us and resumed the conversation, now that her job was done.

Darwish came back. He had made a grand tour of the neighbourhood, and was beaming broadly. I told him about the session that I had just been privileged to see, and he told me more. 'It happens every day, people come, women, and men too. But you haven't seen anything. Do you know her specialism?' I didn't know that there were specialisms in Bedouin folk medicine. Darwish went on to inform me in sign language, and all my young women friends gathered round to help translate and sing Fatma's praises. 'My wife is the specialist in breathing. When you have pains in the throat, and often in the head as well, you come and she goes to work. She gives your neck a vigorous massage, then she presses on your palate to make you bring up all the infections stuck in your throat, till you bleed.' I imagined the scene, but I don't know whether, if I had throat pains, I would have the courage to put myself through that kind of shock treatment. But that wasn't all. 'You're already feeling better, but then it's essential for her to brand the top of your skull, or else the sickness returns, and stays.'

'Brand it?' I flinched.

Darwish reassured me — 'No, no, it's not so awful' — and pointed to a little mark on top of his bald head. 'I've had it done, and I haven't had any more throat trouble since.' I told myself that treatment like that must be quite a deterrent, but no one around me took fright. Then again, our terrible chemical medicines can sometimes cause havoc in our bodies, even though the little pills look harmless ... it's all a question of habit, I suppose.

★　★　★

Ten Egyptian pounds, one and a half English pounds, to swim with Olin. All the guides suggest it, and bring their lucky clients to the Muzeini.

Some now come a very long way especially to meet the dolphin. Then they stay on the beach and eat with everybody else. These people do not pay to enter the water, but only for a place to stay and excellent meals, based on grilled fish, at trifling prices compared with those in the industrialized countries. More and more people are turning up like this: Ibrahim calls them 'the backpacks'. 'They carry their house on their back, so many things, I wonder what they're for ... ' It is true that for a Bedouin used to travelling for days with nothing more than a camel and some goatskins it seems funny to have so many tubes of anti-mosquito, anti-perspirant and moisturizing creams, not to mention sunblock, sunglasses, shampoo, warm clothing, shoes and sandals, a groundsheet, sleeping-bag, books, charms and all sorts of souvenirs. Even the medicines seem redundant to Ibrahim: 'I quite understand that they're not at home and they're frightened of illnesses. But they can buy medicine here too ... They tire themselves out by having everything on their backs — it's pointless. The main thing is money: bring money and you can do anything. That's what you need — a bag full of dollars on your back!' Mischievously, he studies my reaction, knowing as he does that these young backpackers think of themselves as penniless. I laugh at his analysis, and answer: 'Yes, but you know, money is too expensive!' We laugh, and he serves me the second glass of tea, the drink of friendship. His handsome face, chiselled by the sun, offers his smile like a treasure. I would not exchange any back-pack for that gift from Ibrahim.

Abid'allah joins us, and Ibrahim briefly signs him our conversation. Abid'allah tells me: 'Yes, some of them are nice, and others no good, it depends.' The Bedouin touchstone for anyone they meet is the human worth they see in that person. They do not value those they consider weak, too easily influenced, or insincere. That is common to all the tribes, and sometimes it derives from a sign, though possibly misinterpreted. But they have respect for everybody, so nothing comes of these occasionally hasty judgements, which in any case can change over time.

Cautiously, I ask Ibrahim how, with their legendary tradition of hospitality, Bedouins perceive the waves of tourists. 'Ah! Well of course, it changes things. Among us, everyone can turn up when they want. Imagine, you're in the desert, you're lost. You come across a tent, and straight away the people inside are your hosts, they'll give you all they have, food and drink, help on your way, everything. It's the same in the village. But you mustn't stay for more than three and a half days. That is the rule. Do you see? After that, it's very rude, and you're imposing. It's logical, right?'

'Well, of course it's logical. You've got to feed the family first, guests aren't everything.'

Ibrahim pauses: 'So you see, in the beginning we didn't make visitors pay, then little by little we realized that tourists didn't understand that, it's our tradition, at home they pay taxes on everything. So we have to do the same, otherwise they ruin us without intending to, one after another . . . There you are!'

Ibrahim cites one of his friends. 'Look at Martin. Well, to start with I wondered what this . . . let's say this dreamer . . . was doing among our people, sitting there for days on end. He had a silly grin, he knew nothing about our ways, he was always putting his foot in it . . . Pascale, you've no idea how much he got on my nerves!' Abid'allah nods — 'He's a good guy' — and Ibrahim goes on: 'Today, we are friends. I realized that he was sincere. So never mind if he's a little bit strange for us, because it's as if he's at home there, as if he had no house of his own, no family, no money, really no standing anywhere, you understand. He doesn't seem to matter to anybody. Here that's unknown. Among us, everyone has his place.' I think of the impression I make on Ibrahim and Abid'allah. In their minds, I have a house, a husband, a job, I obviously have money because I own a car. So I'm respectable. Not only that, but I travel, and I already know a lot of foreign countries and speak their languages, I can get by all over the world, which fascinates Fatma in particular.

Once again, Abid'allah seems to read my mind: 'You'll come back to see us soon, won't you?' This invitation cuts short all my questions, but I simply reply, 'Of course,' with thanks in my eyes for my two friends.

We pour ourselves the third glass of tea, the tea of life.

Nuweiba el Muzeina village, June 1997

Abid'allah visited the big building site of his hotel several times a day. He gave his verdict on progress to the Egyptian builders in his own way, by shouting in their ears. They knew that his hearing was poor, so they were bound to excuse him. His friends and neighbours could tell from his attitude that he was also getting a bit of his own back — he, the respected client, who once had to be kept and protected.

Every day he changed details from the original plan, and forced the labourers to step up their usual pace. But I think this was genuine; he is continually restless, always changing and rearranging, and to him there is nothing strange about having a different hotel in his mind from one moment to the next.

It was late spring, and not too hot — thirty degrees in the shade, maybe more. The trowels and plumb levels were busy, the Egyptian workers resigned. The staircase rose step by step, the concrete spread and set. In just a few weeks, the hotel's skeleton was standing, still rough from having grown so

229

quickly, but rising above the bare sand between the foot of the date palms and the sea. Over to one side, the wooden doors and window frames waited their turn.

Abid'allah had handed over the last of his cash to the architect. Now he had nothing left to pay the next week's wages, or even buy materials. He explained to the foreman, who already understood: 'We'll have to wait a bit. As soon as I've saved another thousand, I'll call you back.' The mouhendis nodded his head. Here in Egypt it is not unusual, and actually quite common, for sites to stand idle for lack of money, then for work to start again when enough has been put aside. The architect and workers, all paid by the day, may feel practically sure that they will never see their client again, but that is the way of things.

So in the middle of Muzeina beach, next to the little stone cabin, stood a house of raw concrete, with big vaulted rooms and empty windows gaping out to sea. Abid'allah's hotel. For the clans of Muzeina it was more than an outward sign of wealth, it was a sceptre, a symbol. This beach is no longer a piece of waste ground, and Abid'allah is no longer the boy with problems but a proud man that everybody listens to. He owns the only 'hotel' in the village, and what a mansion it is!

From then on, the beach became dotted with huts, at a rate of two or three a month. Each family wanted to use its seaside plot to cash in on Muzeina's new ecotourism, this unexpected dolphin rush. Muhammad was one of the first to build a few small huts, with walls of woven reeds and palm-leaf roofs. The beaten earth was covered with Chinese cotton rugs. Each hut has its own door and small wooden window, to guarantee privacy.

The showers are public, and sometimes they run out of water. The best way to wash is to use the old facilities, concrete cubicles where you take turns to empty buckets of water brought beforehand from the well over the person hidden from sight inside. Like all devotees of the Sinai and its rustic tourism, I prefer these open-top showers, with their plentiful fresh water. No floods, no blocked drains, but plenty of giggles, because it isn't always easy to sluice a bather blindly, over a wall.

Muzeina village, summer 1997

The night conceals its moon and myriad stars, and uncovers the Jordanian mountains across the sea. They stand out against a soft and overcast sky, to put in a furtive appearance before being swallowed for the rest of the day by the veil of heat and dust and the dazzling opacity of the sun.

The horizon is a line that hems this veil to show the sea, whose wavelets shimmer with shifting blues. The surface lapping hints at a deeper order, logic, movement — a serene, innocuous lapping that conceals the sound and fury of another world. The undersea deeps are a planet apart, with its own countryside and towns, pleasures and disasters, parasites and workers, and non-stop activity so little known to humans that sometimes they would rather ignore it.

★   ★   ★

Out of the deeps that morning came Jimmy, to greet Abid'allah. Seasons, rain and the blazing sun seemed not to affect him. He frisked on the reef in barely seventy centimetres of water. Olin still kept a close eye on all his antics, because at six months he was too young to look after himself, even around these humans who watched him like one of their own. Ramadan also arrived, and the party began. He splashed Jimmy while his elder brother slipped off to find Olin. She waited, unmoving, just a few metres away. Falah joined Ramadan, and their revels shook the date palms on the shore, and fetched the tourists out of their huts. Like the elfin bells in fairy tales, the children's laughter mingled with the water's, and splashed the beach with pleasure.

These rarest of mornings in Muzeina dissolve all the troubles in life. Abid'allah goes out to fish for his friend's daily ration. He will be back in a few hours' time, long before nightfall. Muhammad to one side of the beach, and Ibrahim ten metres further on, see to their respective guests and huts. The aroma of coffee with cardamom spices the sea spray for a moment. It is one of the sovereign cures for any tiredness.

The Western-style breakfast has broken out in this little world of Nuweiba el Muzeina, with new-laid egg omelettes, fromage blanc, cereals and the compulsory wheaten pancakes with honey. I wonder what Breton cook has passed this way. I had never seen such dishes here till now! Before, the Middle Eastern hummus, chickpea and fava bean paste, grilled fish, mixed salad with olive oil, and sometimes a little lebne, goat's milk fromage blanc, were on the menu at any time of day. Lamb and camel meat were reserved for celebrations. Not to mention the delicious bottled guava juice made in Egypt.

After the morning meal and the conversations between Dutch, Belgian and American tourists, who make themselves acquainted in English, some decide to go swimming, others prefer to settle in the shade and unwind at the Bedouin tempo. Muhammad is alert to all his guests' wishes, and tries to anticipate their needs. This difficult exercise suits him. And no one wants for anything. He has even bought anti-mosquito coils, ready to be lit in the huts at night, because pale Dutch skin seems to attract them inexorably.

But suddenly that day, as the sultry weather set in, the children playing in the water started to scream. It was ten o'clock. Muhammad was busy in the kitchen, and did not see the uproar breaking out on the beach. One of his guests, who had been there for several days, rushed in and made urgent gestures, pointing first at the dolphin painted on the wall, then towards the sea.

An unrecognizable Muhammad, his mouth, eyes and nose a blank, as if erased by fear, strode towards the beach. In shorts and T-shirt he made for the reef, towards the group of agitated children. All in a rush, they deluged him with signs, but from Ramadan's tearful eyes, as he floated there like a piece of lifeless driftwood, he realized that something serious had happened to Jimmy. The dolphin calf was lying on the sand at the bottom, only this time it was not a game. He was shaking like a leaf, and that was his only sign of life. Olin circled frantically around him, but without trying to bring him up for air, though this had to be done, and at once. Muhammad shot to the surface and signed to the children to help; they all dived together, five metres down to where Jimmy was lying. Somehow they managed to raise the bulky, motionless body, which already weighed nearly a hundred kilos, but even on the surface Jimmy no longer moved or breathed. His trembling subsided. His blowhole had closed, for ever. He was dead.

On shore, the tourists didn't know whether this was a bad joke or the real thing. It was all too much, too senseless, too hard. Only an hour ago, Jimmy had been splashing the children with his flippers and Muzeina was paradise. In paradise, nobody dies, it just isn't done.

Muhammad had vanished. The stay-at-home who never leaves his beach and his guests had gone far into the desert, to weep.

★ ★ ★

Jimmy's body was placed in the shade, on a rug. His skin was smooth, perfect, his belly blue and white. Sitting beside him, Ramadan wept and waited. He was waiting for his friend to affirm his presence, the way he had that morning. The other children drifted aimlessly around, from the reef to the beach, and to Jimmy's body. They didn't know what to do with their grief. All they had left of him was the graffiti scrawled over the walls of a few houses, and in the mountains the beautiful rock drawings done by the two boys Falah and Ramadan, now holding each other's hands for reassurance, in case they should lose each other.

Someone had telephoned Dolphin Reef, and Maya promised to get there as soon as she could. She always keeps her word, and in the mind of the Muzeini, right then she was their only hope — but hope of what? Perhaps of understanding what had happened to the young dolphin. Abid'allah of course still knew nothing, and they could only wait for his return to tell him the terrible news.

★   ★   ★

Several hours later, Maya overtook the Jeep loaded with fish that Abid'allah was driving back to the village. They stopped and greeted each other. By the smile on his face, Maya realized that he knew nothing. She told him simply: 'Muhammad sent for me. Something has happened in the village.' Knowing that they send for Maya about dolphin problems and nothing else, Abid'allah turned pale and murmured 'Olin, Olin . . . '

The two vehicles drove in convoy through the dust raised by the Sinai's bumpy roads. The high-tension cable that linked them was invisible.

★ ★ ★

The village looked like a half-dismantled stage set, with people roaming around and talking under their breath. The sun was unbearable, the salt spat out by the sea was repellent, the whole place looked dirty and untidy. Abid'allah howls of rage must have carried as far as St Catherine's monastery. He was convinced that he could have prevented the tragedy. 'I saved him once before, by giving him the kiss of life. I might have done it again, I should have been called.' Abid'allah was well aware that no one knew where he had gone fishing, and that time was short in such a situation, but his sadness had been instantly transformed into a frightful, ungovernable rage. While he paced wildly, ranting and waving his arms, Maya knelt down and examined Jimmy's body. 'Not a trace, nothing. His skin is perfect, he hasn't been wounded. His blowhole is normal, and his fins.' Maya opened his rostrum, counted his teeth, and generally examined the youngster. 'He was in good shape, he didn't hurt himself, didn't choke, I have absolutely no idea what happened.' She added as she rose to her feet: 'Abid'allah, I'm so sorry.' Abid'allah's anger broke. He threw himself into Maya's arms, and the tears poured down their faces until their shirts were wet with their tears.

★ ★ ★

Maya stayed overnight with her friends, to investigate the cause of little Jimmy's death. Together, seated on cushions under the palm-leaf roof of Abid'allah's restaurant, they talked, speculated and reflected. In their glasses, the tea tasted as bitter as life. No tourists intruded on their meeting. The children also kept their distance, for fear of Abid'allah's anger or out of respect for the grown-ups' conversation. Everyone found it incredible that the dolphin could have died for no reason. Muhammad had reappeared that morning, as silently as he had left. He was the only one to offer a plausible explanation, though Maya did not seem very convinced. He reported in sign language, and young Salem translated into Hebrew, 'I believe that food poisoning killed Jimmy. I have my reasons, just you listen. A week ago, a big black ray threatened him. Olin attacked it and drove it off, but she got stung. It was Abid'allah who took the spine out of Olin's stomach himself.' Abid'allah nodded, and indicated a length of fifteen centimetres: 'I even thought that she was injured . . . but, *Alhamdulillah*, she was fine.' Muhammad continued, keen to convince his friends: 'Olin's milk was poisoned by the venom from the ray, and Jimmy drank it several times a day, for six days, and it poisoned him too . . . ' Silence fell on the group while they considered this. Muhammad seemed at least to have found a cause for the young dolphin's sudden death. To reinforce his explanation he added: 'When I fished him out, he was shuddering all over and Olin did nothing to help him . . . as if she understood, isn't that strange?' Maya remained dubious: 'Maybe we'll never know what killed the youngster. I can take a sample to the laboratory in Elat, or Oz's department in Haifa, and try to determine the cause of death . . . if you agree.' The silence thickened. Then Abid'allah rose to his feet. 'That's agreed. You make what studies you want, and we will take care of Olin . . . ' The others were silent. If 'father' agrees, why make objections, they were thinking. The meeting broke up, and Maya took a specimen back to the lab, over the frontier, while Jimmy was buried in the desert, not far from the reef where he lived his life and enchanted so many.

★ ★ ★

On that day of mourning, the Red Sea revealed a new mystery: two dolphins appeared in the distance and waited beyond the reef. Perhaps they were there to console Olin for the loss of Jimmy . . . ? Slowly she glided out to join them, and three proud dorsal fins receded into the distance. On the beach, surprise mingled with sadness: what were they doing there, that day of all days, so close to the reef?

The two dolphins stayed on for three days, to comfort Olin, or else to persuade her — unsuccessfully — to leave with them for good, back to her dolphin life . . . Or perhaps it was just chance that had brought them?

The lab tests in Elat yielded no results. The biologists' conclusion was that, like 25 per cent of his fellow dolphins, Jimmy had died before he was one year old of what they call 'sudden death' syndrome, which is specific to the young. But Muhammad and Ibrahim continued to believe that he was poisoned by his mother's milk, temporarily contaminated by the black ray's venom. To me, a non-expert, this explanation seems very plausible. It might account for the trembling that Muhammad observed before Jimmy finally stopped breathing.

★ ★ ★

Abid'allah was with Olin, in the water, trying to console her and to console himself . . . He tried to feed her, but even by his side in the water she refused the fishes he offered, rejecting them time after time. Abid'allah was desperate, afraid that she would waste away and once again become the starving creature that he had met three years before. She had to eat, but coaxing and stroking weren't working. Abid'allah was compelled to postpone his attempts, and consented to let her mourn for a while — a few days at most.

But next day and the following days Olin flatly refused all the fish Abid'allah brought, and he became so affected, so crushed, that despite his legendary pride he admitted that he needed his friends' support: he asked Muhammad to try to feed Olin. Muhammad was certain this wouldn't work. In his view, she was not angry but afraid. He was convinced that she blamed these fish for poisoning and killing her young. She had after all accepted some squid. So squid became Olin's staple diet.

Squid are hard for Olin to flush out on her own, because they hide and cling beneath the rocks on the sea bottom. Around Muzeina, it now gets very difficult to find octopus among the undersea rocks. Olin consumes so many that it has upset the natural balance of the local fauna. Abid'allah and Muhammad have decided to keep her supplied with it as long as they can, but now find themselves pushed to meet the demand. Sometimes Abid'allah brings a few back from his fishing trips. And when he returns empty-handed, it is the children's and sometimes the village women's job to use crowbars to dislodge the big octopuses, thirty or forty centimetres in diameter, that lurk out of sight on the reef.

One day, after removing the harmful ink sac from the squid, Abid'allah remembered the big show they used to put on before Olin was pregnant, and before Jimmy came along. Every day from then on he went out in his boat, standing up in the bow to hold out her favourite sweetmeat. She would soar to seize the squid as she did before, and when he held it between his teeth her spectacular leap to graze Abid'allah's mouth looked like a kiss of love.

More miracles

Nuweiba el Muzeina village,
September 1997

Hearing talk about a little foreign girl who had visited that summer, I questioned Abid'allah, and he laughed at my prying. 'You want to know it all! Her name is Heidi, and she's this tall' — he held his hand out eighty centimetres above the ground. 'But ask Ibrahim, he'll tell you everything! I have an appointment . . . ' I might as well have finished his sentence for him — he didn't have the patience to sit telling stories. I surrendered, and Ibrahim joined me, ordering a glass of tea.

'The month of August 1997 is hot. Muzeina is tired and sleepy in the sun. Heidi is nine years old and she intends to shake our pretty beach out of its tropical daze. First, I'll describe her. Heidi's sight is poor, she hears very little, and she doesn't walk, just crawls around on all fours, like a baby, you see. She doesn't speak, and she dribbles down her chin when she's tired. Heidi was born with a serious malformation, and none of the

243

doctors can help, back home in Switzerland. They prescribe drugs to improve her concentration, and she follows all the therapy required, but her condition doesn't really improve.'

Heidi and her parents were new guests at the Mekhassen hotel in Nuweiba el Muzeina. They had several weeks' holiday to spend, and their intention was to take Heidi to swim in the sea for the very first time, and gradually to introduce her to Olin.

'You know Abid'allah,' Ibrahim went on. 'He didn't pay any attention to this child and her special needs. Too busy, and lost in his grief, with both eyes fixed on Olin's health. All the same, like all the tourists, they went bathing on the Muzeina reef — right here!' He pointed five metres out from the beach.

Heidi had a rubber ring, and although she felt nervous she was safe. The young Bedouins were very intrigued by this odd child, and plenty of curious glances came her way. At the start, Heidi was afraid of them, but slowly they all got used to the new situation, and with help from her mother Heidi could stay there in the middle of all those very noisy children's games.

Heidi responded very rarely to what went on around her, and only by crying. It was as if it was only troubles she perceived, and never joy. She communicated with no one, and never met anyone's eye, not even her mother's. Several times a day she was taken down to the sea, and at first she would scream every time. She felt distressed by all that salt water in motion, a whole new element. But her mother and father insisted, so like it or not she got used to the new environment. The Bedouins in Muzeina were very patient with these untypical tourists, and day by day they became more involved in the beach's life.

After a week, Heidi's father decided that it was time. He took his daughter further out to meet Olin, still wearing her rubber ring. At once, the dolphin seemed to take an interest in the odd child. She quickly approached her on the surface, in reach of her hand, to let herself be stroked. But the child had too little control of her movements to move closer, and anyway, did she want to? A few Bedouins gathered on the beach with startled looks. Olin was not in the habit of approaching strangers so readily. To them, this marked the birth of a fine new story. But they didn't know Heidi and her problems.

Late next morning, Abid'allah entered the water to rendezvous with Olin, pet her, and check that she hadn't lost weight, his obsession since Jimmy's death. Heidi was there with her mother, wearing her rubber ring, and Olin was circling around them. Abid'allah had heard about what happened the day before.

He swam closer, and brought the dolphin to greet the girl. Olin utterly surrendered to the child, who started to make vague onomatopoeic noises for the first time. Was she trying to make contact with Olin? Was she communicating joy? Nobody knew, but in any case she was at least expressing her feelings some other way than crying, and soon her mother had tears in her eyes.

Each day brought its share of ups and downs. Abid'allah was astonished the next day when Heidi instead started to scream as soon as he and Olin came near, and refused even the most distant contact. Her father explained that she needed a lot of time to assimilate anything new, and that disheartening setbacks always followed signs of progress. This news came as a sad surprise to all the friends on the beach — Salem, Muhammad and Abid'allah — who were ready to help their guest however they could.

On the morning of the twentieth day, the growing girl ate a big breakfast. Abid'allah came to say hello. Like all the Muzeini, he spoke to her in the same slightly simplified local sign language that they use with me. In any case, Heidi did not hear words, and anyway they would have to have been in Swiss German. She was her usual huddled and apathetic self, so much so that you couldn't help wondering whether her parents might not be suffering from wishful thinking. Abid'allah sat in the shade of the palm-leaf roof, drinking his coffee, chatting with the mother and the few guests in his hotel. Then Heidi put her hand on his knee.

Usually Heidi's movements were clumsy and seemed purposeless, but now she looked up at Abid'allah, raised the hand, and made the sign for 'dolphin' so clearly that it couldn't be mistaken. A wave of feeling swamped Abid'allah, who didn't wait, but picked up the child, hugged her, and took her off to swim with Olin. Heidi's excited mother held out the rubber ring, but Abid'allah wanted nothing to come between the girl and Olin, nothing but the start of the same communication that now comes so easily to him.

From that day on, Heidi never again felt afraid of the sea, or Olin, or Abid'allah. She created a potential link, or at any rate the first to be visible and clearly expressed. Each morning, Abid'allah took her out into the water, and in the fourth week Heidi, held in his arms, caressed Olin — she who had never shown a hint of affection to anyone, and appeared to take no interest in anything. To Heidi's overjoyed parents, it was clear that her budding relationship with Olin was achieving kinds of progress that they called '*ein Wunder*' — a miracle.

In the days that followed, Heidi gradually stood up straighter to limp to the water's edge and meet her dolphin. Before, she only used to walk during her physio sessions in Switzerland. At home, she had never taken a single spontaneous step. But her longing to join Olin really motivated her. By now she had learned other signs that her clumsy hands were already rehearsing, and she managed to communicate with her parents without crying, even though tears remained her first resort. Her mother was tempted to stay on with her to reinforce her progress, but they had to go back and resume their life in Switzerland.

Ibrahim concluded: 'We think we'll see Heidi and her parents next year, maybe even sooner. The child was too happy here for them to forget us.'

★   ★   ★

Maya explains that dolphins probably have no therapeutic powers as such, but only a gift that affects humans in particular, a gift to charm them and lift their spirits very fast. 'In the presence of dolphins, people often give the best of themselves,' comments Sophie, who runs Dolphin Reef's therapeutic support programme. 'I've seen very contained and also very stressed kinds of people open up to dolphins in a few seconds, and be transformed. First, the sea has its own relaxing powers. And the ambassador dolphin has that smile that charms us even if we know that it's permanent, and has nothing to do with how it feels. And then we're fascinated by its eyes, and by its movements, all that power and resilience combined.' I enthuse: 'Dolphins are gorgeous, that's all!' Sophie hesitates: 'It's not only that. The dolphin is a wild animal. Unfortunately we usually meet it in captivity, but basically it's still an untamed animal. So we're meeting a nature that we mostly know nothing about. And when the dolphin lets us touch it, then as I see it another dimension comes into play.' My questioning glance fetches a smile: 'Touch it is a very powerful therapeutic medium. And this is the key feature in the dolphin way of life. They constantly touch each other, for the slightest reason, and they love to touch and be touched by the humans they allow inside their personal circle. That exchange is a fantastic experience. For twenty years it has been demonstrated that certain sound frequencies emitted by dolphins directly increase the output of endorphins in our bodies. These are chemical substances that produce a kind of mild euphoria and good humour in humans, and relieve all kinds of pain. So when dolphins help humans, there's that much at least going on.' Now I begin to understand what I felt when Jimmy looked me straight in the eye. He may have bombarded my brain with a frequency that boosted my alpha waves and left me feeling blissful in less than a minute. Some wild animal!

Abid'allah's thinking is more down-to-earth. 'Olin helps people, of course! Here, every day you can learn about some new experience, from a story told by someone who has gone swimming with Olin.' He pauses to think for a moment, and adds very seriously: 'But most of all she helps me, Abid'allah!' He goes on: 'You know, last year an American woman, or maybe Australian, I don't remember, came with a group of friends. You weren't here. She was a little bit afraid of Olin, but all the same she wanted to see her up close. When she swam near her, she didn't want to leave the water, and after a few hours her friends called out for her to come back to the hotel to collect her stuff and catch the flight back. But she wouldn't listen, she was staying with Olin. The plane, the plane, they were panicked. So they used force to catch her, and hauled her into the taxi, still in her swimsuit. You didn't know whether to laugh or cry. To miss her plane ... ' He smiles, and reminds me: 'You see how people love Olin, unbelievable. It isn't just me!'

★   ★   ★

Muhammad asked Abid'allah if he had told me the story about the Italian. Abid'allah laughed again. 'Ah, the Italian, what a fright he gave us!' Then he stopped: sometimes he loves to be coaxed. 'I went out diving with a family of Italians. We were in the water, and no sign of Olin! She seemed to have disappeared ... but you know, when I'm in the water with friends, she sneaks in and pressed against me. And in fact she suddenly turns up facing the father of the family. He was hypnotized, as if he'd been struck by lightning. Nose to nose with Olin, neither of them moving, not a twitch. I was so frightened. He'd stopped breathing, and I thought he was having a heart attack. I raised his head above the water, then I pulled him out of the sea, with his family right behind me, like a parcel. He was heavy. He kept on whispering, '*Delfino . . . Delfino.*' Imagine, a big guy like that.' Abid'allah swelled his chest and stuck out his flat stomach to imitate him. 'He'd had a bad shock because of Olin, and I was really scared. It took him a day to recover, and his wife refused to stay here!'

What a clown! He mimed the scene. His energy — top gear from morning to night — is infectious, when it isn't totally exhausting! He can't keep still for an instant, plans ten things at once, works like a Trojan, fishes, dives, sells, buys, talks, travels . . . and still has time for Olin and his friends . . . I think of his future wife, if he should marry. Poor woman, what a dance he'd lead her.

Nuweiba el Muzeina village, January 1998

The children race from house to house and yard to yard, all along the beach. They are spreading the news: old Mekhassen and Abid'allah's aunt have been seen visiting little Jamia's parents with the *mansaf*, the ceremonial marriage proposal tray. As for Abid'allah Mekhassen, he has disappeared, busy evading questions in the mountains. He still chooses the desert to be on his own, because above all, like all Muzeini, his deepest attachment is to the Sinai and its rocks. For them it is the only peaceful place in the world.

So Abid'allah is to marry, much to the surprise of the other villagers, who are astonished not to have heard any rumours. In Muzeina, everything is surmised, known and turned into fact, long before anything at all has happened.

Abid'allah has been old enough to marry for some time, but it is getting harder and harder for the men of the tribe to take a wife. Fatma explained to me that in the old days the suitor had to present his betrothed with a goat-hair tent, some cooking-pots, and one or several camels. Today, it takes a solid house, some furniture, the kitchen utensils, TV, a stove and even a washing machine. Some parents also ask for the traditional *mahr* for their daughter, money to buy gold jewellery that will make up the rest of her personal fortune. A dowry can vary among the Muzeini from one to four thousand Egyptian pounds (about a hundred and fifty to six hundred pounds sterling), a fortune for them. The men have to save for several years to get married, and they start their families, as in many Arab countries nowadays, later and later. It is a real problem for society, because these men are now inured to their bachelor life, and it comes hard to make the compromises necessary for living as a couple. Worse, they grow sour during all those years of loneliness; and isolation. Bedouin society is made for families; bachelors are loose ends among them and soon feel unhappy. Muhammad tells me that he has been saving up to take a wife. He is twenty-four already, and longing to build a family. For Juma it is even more complicated, because he doesn't seem to have a penny to his name.

The Jamia in question is eighteen years old, slender and pretty, with all the self-assurance of the women of Muzeina, who know very young what they want out of life. Under her veil of black muslin embroidered with gold and held tight, I sense her dark and silky hair. It sways against the slightly transparent tulle, and reaches to her waist. Gilded pearls highlight the cheerful brilliance of her kohl-rimmed eyes. She is very proud that Abid'allah is attracted to her; her expression is radiant. And if she seems reserved, like most girls of marriageable age, our talks in Fatma's patio reveal her humour and independent spirit. Abid'allah did not choose by chance. As I see it, they are well matched, and there will be fire in their partnership.

Settling the future

Three years ago, only the Mekhassens' building stood in the middle of the beach, a few metres from the sea. Today, at the foot of the palm-trees, around the big whitewashed hotel, a string of four small cafés with adjoining huts occupies about thirty metres of beach.

This year, still banned from driving, and fed up with being unemployed, the two deaf brothers Ahmed and Darwish Suleiman decided to build their own tourist complex, the fifth on the beach. On the land inherited from their father, they put up three huts around a little shack that will be the kitchen and restaurant, on the lines of the other cafés on the beach, and very like Abid'allah's pioneering café, now managed, very effectively, by his brother.

Muhammad was furious. His deaf friends were creating more competition, when it was already hard enough to earn a living. He felt betrayed.

Lying on the rugs of his candlelit

restaurant, he complained: 'Every family wants its cut of the loot! But who has looked after Olin every day since she arrived? When Jimmy was small, and somebody had to call Dolphin Reef for help, or to answer questions, or when it came to teaching tricks to Olin, all that was Abid'allah and me, and nobody else!' He was upset, and I understood his feelings, but the Suleimans too needed to earn some money . . . Fair shares are not easy to decide, especially when so much of the little money that comes to Muzeina goes straight to Abid'allah, the famous one. Abid'allah tried to console him. 'Everyone is entitled to a share, we're a whole clan living here, a dozen families, we can't keep it all between the two of us . . . ' Muhammad nodded, but sourly. He feels overlooked, because he thinks that no one has truly recognized his regular work with Olin, and all the credit goes to Abid'allah. He lacks the drive and charisma of his childhood friend. But the next day would be a brighter day for him. And the friendship of Abid'allah and Juma, and the presence of Olin and a few tourists passing through will take his mind off his worries.

★　★　★

The night was dark that evening, its thickness tangible. Without a candle, I could hardly see my hand. I let my eyes unfocus, and they adjusted to its ebony colour. A fragile gibbous moon, set in a field of twinkling diamonds, hung above us, almost in fingertip reach, but I didn't try.

A few metres away, Abid'allah was stretched out under a pile of blankets. Beyond him was Juma, and then Asher. Muhammad signed goodnight. The sea foam turned silver in the moonlight. I lay down, tired out by the day, while the waves teased the pebbles at the end of my small foam mattress. The incoming tide lulled my mind, and my heavy eyelids closed on the quiet stars of the Sinai. I dreamed about the legend of the golden dolphin, and all those gods of mythology who turn into dolphins: Apollo and Vishnu, the myths of the Dogons of Mali and the aborigines of Australia, the Awal totem of the Kwakiutl Indians in Canada ... I dreamed of all those dolphins in the world embodied in Olin, who was swimming out there, just a few metres from my sleeping-bag, at the foot of my silent beach, in the Red Sea.

In the morning, I was hardly awake before the voice of Mayol's book whispered: 'Deep inside oneself, there is calm. Deep inside calm, there is love. It is dolphins who taught me this. It is thanks to them that I have beaten all my records.'

That morning was the moment of reconciliation. As soon as the sun was up, the elders called a meeting. The Suleimans, Ahmed and his father, old Mekhassen, Uncle Ibrahim and his supporter Madane . . . they all came to take tea and to attend this vital gathering. Sheikh Ramadan began by stressing that 'only an agreement today can hold the clan together inside the tribe in Muzeina. Because of outside events, we are starting to hate each other for no good reason. This has to stop.' Old Mekhassen chipped in: 'And this question involves all the families equally.' Yes, but all the same it is the Mekhassens who are the first affected, because everyone agrees that Olin remains in Muzeina because of Abid'allah. They are both the most criticized, because they receive the lion's share of the business centred on Olin, Allah's gift, and also the most admired, because without them neither the dolphin nor the tourists would take the slightest interest in their beach.

The discussion was less heated than usual, because this was no time for petty squabbles. Madane recalled the three great values of the desert: honour, endurance and hospitality. There was no question of discarding thousands of years of civilization and unity among the cross-border clans, tribes and brotherhoods of this vast region for the sake of a few scraps of land, or a dolphin, or even, of course, for money. All the wise men were agreed on reaching compromises. That serious day was a good one for the Muzeini, who handle all crises with a sense of pacifism that others should find inspiring. In the end they decided to share the beach, respecting the divisions of property by family — the same system which has been in existence for centuries.

Nuweiba el Muzeina village, 18 June 1998

Abid'allah's wedding was a great celebration, and I would say the crowning of his destiny. Abid'allah, the young husband, soon to be a father, will be established for good as one of the pillars of his village, and its representative face. Forgotten is the touchy, hyperactive little misfit that no one took notice of. King of not only his feast but his village, his opinion is now more respected than those of the elders who willingly defer to him. The whole clan attended, as well as many foreign guests, such as Asher, Maya and the friends from

Dolphin Reef, Itamar Grinberg the photographer, Oz Goffman the cetologist, and even some worthies from the other tribes of the Sinai, whose presence hinted at a change of status for the deaf of the banished clan. Hundreds of people shared ten fat sheep roasted over charcoal. The women of the two families had been cooking for a week, and the cost of the feast was outrageous, to match the couple's joy. Jamia's face had an expression so full of love that it touched the hardest hearts. The young women of marriageable age showed glimpses of the reds and yellows of their dresses, half hidden under the veils of black tulle that hung all the way down to their gleaming sandals. Their hands, marvellously painted with flowers of kohl, in the Yemeni style, and their eyes both embraced Jamia, and their young mouths too, through her muslin. They shared the hope of making an equally fine, equally happy marriage. Their friends and all the villagers had tears in their eyes at the sight of little Abid'allah leaving with his bride, riding on his decorated camel, amid the cheers and applause, and followed and blessed by Olin, her dorsal fin cutting through the waves along the coast.

First day of the feast of Ramadan, Friday 18 January 1999

Olin has given birth to Ramadan, a male calf in perfect health.

Abid'allah is happy. His human eyes rove across a changing sky on to the beach, with its contours shaped and reshaped by the tides, then on to the restless sea, and on to Olin, who appeared there some years ago, and has stayed there, blessed by Allah, and by men.

Epilogue

I am travelling far from Muzeina, far from its red rock and turquoise water. Over the roads, from the Sinai to the Negev, hangs the hazy regret of parting.

I think about Olin, Abid'allah, Muzeina, and the Gulf of Elat. They are my vision of a coming new world, where men and dolphins freely respect and love each other both for their differences, and for their likenesses.

There are Olin and her little Ramadan, high among the Muzeini, the ten cetaceans of Dolphin Reef, in their enclosure permanently open to the high seas. And present too are the hundreds of thousands of dolphins in the Red Sea, still nameless to us . . .

Theirs is a vision of a peaceful future where, as in their undersea domain, cultures and friendships live without frontiers.

Acknowledgements

My warmest thanks to those whose friendship and experience has shown me a new world:

The whole tribe in Muzeina, and particularly Abid'allah and Jamia Mekhassen, Muhammad Atwa, Juma Aslim, Ahmed, Darwish and Fatma Suleiman, Ibrahim Mekhassen, Salem Muhammad, Madane Salem, Ramadan Ibrahim and Falah Saba.

All the members of Dolphin Reef in Elat, and especially Maya and Roni Zilber, Nir Avni, Oren Lifschitz, Roberto Donio and Inbal Melamed.

Sophie Donio and her project for supportive therapy with the aid of dolphins.

The Research Laboratory on Dolphin Behaviour, and Frank Veit.

Asher Gal.

Irit Slomka.

Edgar Hoffman.

The park of the Submarine Observatory in Elat.

Oz Goffman, director of the Israel Marine Mammals Research and Assistance Centre.

My friend, photographer and underwater cameraman, Itamar Grinberg.

263

Lastly, my very dear friends Tali and Emmanuel Levy and their children Shy, Yotam and Itaï, without whom this book would have been less fun to write.

We do hope that you have enjoyed reading
this large print book.

Did you know that all of our titles
are available for purchase?

We publish a wide range of high quality
large print books including:
Romances, Mysteries, Classics
General Fiction
Non Fiction and Westerns

Special interest titles available in
large print are:
The Little Oxford Dictionary
Music Book
Song Book
Hymn Book
Service Book

Also available from us courtesy of Oxford
University Press:
Young Readers' Dictionary
(large print edition)
Young Readers' Thesaurus
(large print edition)

For further information or a free
brochure, please contact us at:
Ulverscroft Large Print Books Ltd.,
The Green, Bradgate Road, Anstey,
Leicester, LE7 7FU, England.
Tel: (00 44) 0116 236 4325
Fax: (00 44) 0116 234 0205

Other titles in the
Ulverscroft Large Print Series:

STRANGER IN THE PLACE

Anne Doughty

Elizabeth Stewart, a Belfast student and only daughter of hardline Protestant parents, sets out on a study visit to the remote west coast of Ireland. Delighted as she is by the beauty of her new surroundings and the small community which welcomes her, she soon discovers she has more to learn than the details of the old country way of life. She comes to reappraise so much that is slighted and dismissed by her family — not least in regard to herself. But it is her relationship with a much older, Catholic man, Patrick Delargy, which compels her to decide what kind of life she really wants.

DUMMY HAND

Susan Moody

When Cassie Swann is knocked off her bike on a quiet country road, the driver leaves her unconscious and bleeding at the roadside. A man later walks into a police station and confesses, and they gratefully close the case. But something about this guilt-induced confession doesn't smell right, and Cassie's relentless suitor Charlie Quartermain cannot resist doing a little detective work. When a young student at Oxford is found brutally murdered, Charlie begins to suspect that the two incidents are somehow connected. Can he save Cassie from another 'accident' — this time a fatal one?

SAFFRON'S WAR

Frederick E. Smith

Corporal Alan Saffron, ex-aircrew, is desperate to get back into action, but instead he's posted to Cape Town as an instructor, along with Ken Bickers, a friend about as hazardous as an enemy sniper, who considers Saffron a jonah for trouble. Within half an hour of arrival, Saffron's jonah strikes, and he makes an enemy of Warrant Officer Kruger, who turns Saffron's cushy posting into total warfare. With recruits as wild as Hottentots, obsolete aircraft, and Cape Town's infamous watch dog, Nuisance, Saffron's sojourn in South Africa becomes a mixture of adventure, danger and pure hilarity . . .

THE DEVIL'S BRIDE

Penelope Stratton

Lord Rupert Glennister's luck at cards and his tireless sexual appetites were thought to be the work of satanic forces. An outraged society made him an outcast until he could redeem himself by marrying a woman of virtue. Calvina Bracewell was a parson's daughter but was bullied into servitude by her 'benefactors'. Rescued by Lord Rupert, she found herself agreeing to his shocking demand that they should marry that very night. For a while, Calvina was happy but then attempts on her life began. Only one man could want her dead, and that was the husband she'd grown to love.

THE SURGEON'S APPRENTICE

Arthur Young

1947: Young Neil Aitken has worked hard to secure a place at Glasgow University to study medicine. Bearing in mind the Dean's warning that it takes more than book-learning to become a doctor, he sets out to discover what that other elusive quality might be. He learns the hard way, from a host of memorable characters ranging from a tyrannical surgeon to the bully on the farm where Neil works in his spare time, and assorted patients who teach him about courage and vulnerability. Neil also meets Sister Annie, the woman who is to influence his life in every way.